EXCEEDING EXPECTATIONS

The Enterprise Rent-A-Car Story

EXCEEDING EXPECTATIONS

The Enterprise Rent-A-Car Story

STAN BURNS

GREENWICH PUBLISHING GROUP, INC.
LYME, CONNECTICUT

Any omissions are regretted. Corrections sent to the publisher will be included in later editions.

Produced and published by:
Greenwich Publishing Group, Inc., Lyme, Connecticut

Design by Connolly & Connolly, Inc.

Prepress by Silver Eagle Graphics, Inc.

Library of Congress Catalog Card Number: 97-73084

ISBN: 0-944641-23-7

First Printing: October 1997

10 9 8 7 6 5 4 3 2 1

Photography credits:

Page 26	Arteaga Photos, Ltd.
Page 29	Arteaga Photos, Ltd.
Page 30	Arteaga Photos, Ltd.
Page 34 (top right)	Arteaga Photos, Ltd.
Page 35 (top)	Arteaga Photos, Ltd.
Page 35 (bottom)	UPI/Corbis-Bettmann
Page 80	© Paul & Lindamarie Ambrose/ FPG International Corp.
Page 81	UPI/Corbis-Bettmann
Page 82	Pfister Photo Service
Page 85	St. Louis Post-Dispatch
Page 87 (top)	Corbis-Bettmann
Page 87 (middle)	St. Louis Post-Dispatch
Page 87 (bottom)	St. Louis Mercantile Library
Page 88	Missouri Historical Society, St. Louis photo by Ted McCrea
Page 89	St. Louis Mercantile Library
Page 91(right)	Corbis-Bettmann
Page 104	© Joachim Messerschmidt/ FPG International Corp.
Page 107	© The Houston Post Co. photo by Danny Connolly
Pages 114-115	© Travelpix/ FPG International Corp.
Pages 132-133	© Ken Ross/ Viesti Associates, Inc.
Pages 148-149	Corbis-Bettmann
Page 158	© James Randklev/ FPG International Corp.
Page 181 (bottom)	photo by Judy Brinkman

All other pictures courtesy of Enterprise and Enterprise employees; photography of Enterprise artifacts by Timothy J. Connolly.

Dedicated to all members of the Enterprise family — past, present, future.

As we mark the 40th anniversary of the founding of Enterprise, the entire Enterprise family has good reason to celebrate and to reflect. *Exceeding Expectations* was written so that we might all understand our heritage, share our own experiences and more fully appreciate our sense of commitment to each other as we move forward. We believe that as we leave the twentieth century, it is critically important for us to know where we have been so that we can better understand the future.

The early portions of the book tell the stories of our beginnings. These stories are not being retold just for the sake of documenting the historical milestones of Enterprise. More importantly, they help us understand those cultural values that bind us together as a team. Clearly, Jack's earliest business experiences established the principles that have enabled our growth and success to far exceed our wildest dreams. The early stories demonstrate that our principles worked in tough times, and we are confident they will work again on similar occasions in the future.

The book also helps us understand the evolution of the various parts of our business. It demonstrates how our growth has been the result of both an unyielding commitment to the values established early on, and a determination to plan our future with careful attention to the changing world that holds great promise for our future.

This is a book that could go on and on and never be complete. The more stories we share, the more stories we hear. There are many people in the ever-extending Enterprise family whose contributions to the company have been meaningful, but whose names and faces are not recorded here. We are grateful for all of those contributions and proud that the stories in this book are examples of countless similar efforts.

Our hope is that you will enjoy the book and that as you read it, you will feel a deeper sense of connection to all members of the Enterprise family — those who built the foundation that continues to provide secure support for our growth, those who work next to you today and those who we will welcome in the future. Thanks to all of you for making this dream possible!

Andy Taylor
President and Chief Executive Officer

Jack Taylor
Founder and Chairman

Contents

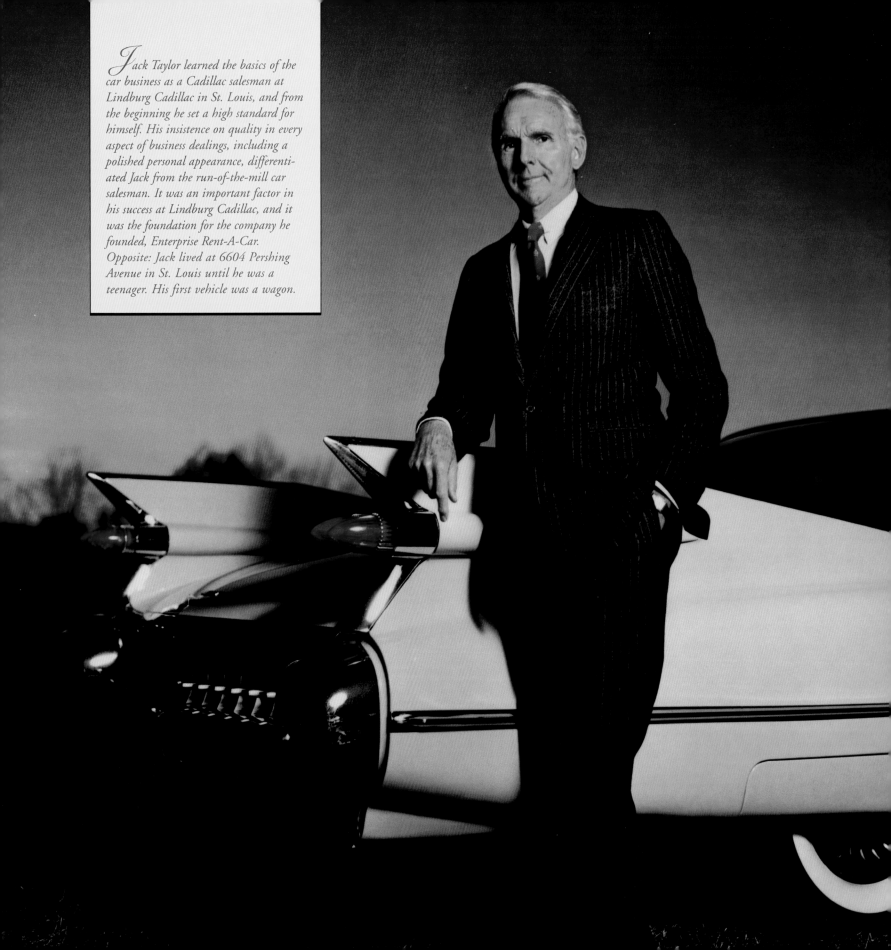

Jack Taylor learned the basics of the car business as a Cadillac salesman at Lindburg Cadillac in St. Louis, and from the beginning he set a high standard for himself. His insistence on quality in every aspect of business dealings, including a polished personal appearance, differentiated Jack from the run-of-the-mill car salesman. It was an important factor in his success at Lindburg Cadillac, and it was the foundation for the company he founded, Enterprise Rent-A-Car.
Opposite: Jack lived at 6604 Pershing Avenue in St. Louis until he was a teenager. His first vehicle was a wagon.

$\mathcal{T}$HE EARLY VISION

"We just thought you were slow, thought that was why school never agreed with you. Fs in every course you took and a B in gym your freshman year in college — the family all figured that you just didn't have it."

Jack Taylor tilted his head back slightly and sat still for a minute, smiling. His high cheekbones and smooth white hair gave him the look of a relaxed gentleman. Then came his unique laugh, a sound that is part belly laugh and part chuckle, a sound that is the delightful signature of a nice guy. "That's what my brother told me," he said as the laugh subsided, and he nodded his head and grinned. "I guess they had reason to think I was slow. I always hated school, and I'm sure my mother knew it and the whole family talked about it."

"Let me tell you the story," Jack said as he took off his glasses and rubbed his eyes and smiled.

I don't know why I hated school, but my family is right about that. As a kid I despised Monday mornings more than anything. I knew the teacher was going to call on me, and I knew I wouldn't get it right. I had knots in my stomach before I got there.

Who knows where that attitude came from — maybe it was just me. I didn't feel any real pressure from my parents. My father was a sweet man who wanted everybody to be happy, and I thought he was great. He was a stockbroker in St. Louis. We lived in Clayton, which is a close suburb of St. Louis. Dad was a good-looking man with an engaging personality and many friends. He and his friends had a good time and laughed a lot. He always tried to avoid confrontations, either at work or at home — he wanted to be happy.

Dad was a laid-back, easygoing guy

Jack's father was Melbourne Martling Taylor, above, a handsome but unpretentious man who was known simply as Mel. Jack's mother, Dorothy Crawford Taylor, right, was born in 1900. She remained close to her parents throughout her life, and they were an important part of Jack's life too. Below is Dorothy as a young girl, with her brother Ellis on the far left.

and was not very aggressive in business. He made a good living, but he didn't push hard. He felt that who you are matters more than how much money you make, and sometimes that seemed to backfire on him.

I remember one time when he put a deal together for a friend — a person he trusted — who was trying to expand his business. Dad's friend was very interested in acquiring another company, and Dad talked with someone he knew out of town who was a likely prospect. He then helped the two men work out the framework for the deal, and because he trusted his friend, Dad didn't specifically discuss

When Jack was 13 the Taylor family moved from Pershing Avenue to 34 Oakleigh Lane. It was a bigger and finer house with ample room for Jack and his brother, Paul, as well as for his grandparents, who moved in with the Taylors. Jack lived in this house until he left home to join the navy.

Mel Taylor had served as an enlisted man in the Marine Corps before he married Dorothy. His military stories were retold many times as Jack and Paul grew up, and the excitement and drama of those stories fueled the dreams of the two young boys.

what might be in it for him. He had assumed he would be treated fairly.

When it was all over and the deal was done, Dad's friend sent him a case of whiskey, or something like that. It was a nice gift, but it certainly wasn't very much in light of the fact that it was Dad who made the whole thing happen. My dad never pushed it. I knew he was disappointed,

but he said to me, "If that's how he wants to handle it, he's the loser, not me. He's losing his integrity." I didn't understand that point of view very much when I was young, but it's clear now that I learned from my dad that who you are and how you act is more important than whether you make a lot of money on a particular deal.

I learned a lot from my father about his attitude toward life and about our family. I have an old family bible that traces the Taylors back to Worcester Taylor, who was born in 1806 and came west from New England. My grandfather was in the fur-trading business, and St. Louis was the center of action for fur traders who went up the Missouri River and brought furs back to the city.

He sold those furs to people in the East, and though I never knew a whole lot about him, I heard people in the family say he was a tough old guy.

Sam Crawford was my mother's father, and he was a successful businessman. He worked for a railroad

11

Jack, at right in the picture above, was 19 months older than Paul, on the left. The age difference was just enough to enable Jack to play the natural role of the big brother, and yet they were close enough in age to play together like friends. Mel and Dorothy fenced in the yard on Pershing Avenue, left, no doubt to make it easier to keep a close eye on both boys.

supply company, which was big business in the late 1800s. He got a couple of patents and was always involved in the manufacturing side of the business. He and I had a certain rapport because I loved things mechanical and so did he — it was his work.

Every morning he got dressed in a suit and tie. He said it made a better impression on people, and it certainly did — especially on me. It was his example that taught me a professional appearance is the mark of a serious businessman. But he was always so focused on his work that he couldn't separate himself from the business. My grandfather's example also showed me that every businessman needs to draw a line between work and the rest of his life. He was always immersed in his work and was very affected by his retirement.

Mother liked the good things in life, and she and Dad spent everything he made — sometimes more than he made. She engineered the plan for my

*S*am and Gertrude Crawford, Jack's grandparents, are pictured here on the boardwalk in Atlantic City in 1936. Sam Crawford had a high-paying job, and Gertrude loved to travel. When Jack and Paul were growing up, Sam and Gertrude often took the boys on trips to Virginia Beach, once sending them both home after only two days because the two rowdy young boys did not meet their grandmother's high standard for decorum. Opposite: This print, What a Great Day, depicts Jack Taylor as a young boy. The original painting by Greg Olsen was meant to convey the satisfaction of an active day and the exciting prospect of tomorrow. The print was distributed to celebrate the 35th anniversary of Enterprise Rent-A-Car.

grandparents to move in with us. Part of her thinking was that they could help financially, and she thought they would be a good influence on two growing boys. Also, there would be more income in the house with my grandparents there. My grandmother took my brother and me shopping every fall for school clothes at Boyd's, an old store in downtown St. Louis,

and she always paid the bill. Another benefit of having my grandparents live with us was that we had enough money to have hired help at home. We had a maid in the kitchen, and there was a tall, quiet man named Theodore who served us dinner. In retrospect, a maid and butler does seem incredible, but as I said, we lived beyond our means.

My grandparents also paid my tuition for a private high school and as much of college as I attended. (My grandmother was a firm believer in the benefits of education.) We had two cars, and we lived comfortably and liked having my grandparents there. It was a happy place to grow up, but even with the help from my grandparents, Dad was always pinched for dough.

There was one incident that has always stayed with me. One night we were at home having dinner. There was a knock on the door, and Theodore came in and told my father that somebody would like to see him. Dad went out, and there was some fussing around.

We could hear them talking but could not hear exactly what was said.

I heard enough to know that the man had come to get a check for the car payment or to take the car. We continued eating, somewhat embarrassed, and then heard Dad go upstairs. I could hear him going through drawers, and then he went out in the front yard and talked to the man again. After a while Dad came back in, sat down and resumed dinner. Not a word was said. He must have come up with enough money to take care of the payment, because the car stayed where it was and was not discussed. I don't know if it bothered Dad, or whether he took it in stride, but that incident stuck in my mind. I said to myself right then that it would never happen to me — and it hasn't. My business philosophy has always embraced being conservative and frugal with money.

Because of our precarious financial situation, I worked and saved money to buy my own car — though I couldn't afford it until after I graduated from high school. To me, it was more than just trans-

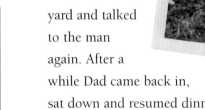

portation. Earl Lindburg, my best friend in high school, and I were both car nuts. Earl's father was the Cadillac distributor and also had dealerships in St. Louis — he always had a new car. Earl would come by and pick me up on Saturday mornings, and we'd buzz

School, sports and dogs were all part of growing up. On the left, Paul is stretched out with Checky, the runt Dalmatian that was part of the Taylor family. Jack attended the Taylor School (a private school with no relationship to Jack's family) from the fifth grade through the eleventh. The entire student body is pictured below, including Paul Taylor, who under the school's policy towards siblings could attend free as long as Jack paid full tuition. Jack's close friend Earl Lindburg was also at the Taylor School during those years, though Jack transferred to Clayton High School for his senior year when the Taylor School discontinued the sibling "discount."

14

JACK   MEL   PAUL

talked about showed up.) I left Washington University after one semester in the spring of 1941, never having felt a strong sense of commitment to academic studies.

I had always liked things mechanical and loved to tinker with cars and drive fast, so after the attack on Pearl Harbor, I decided to enlist in the service and become a pilot. The army rejected me because I had hay fever, so I tried the navy. They told me I had to take a test. I really panicked because taking tests reminded me of school, and I had never done well on tests in school. But for the first time, I was motivated to get a good grade — I was excited about the prospect of being a navy pilot. I took the test and passed it. I think it was sheer determination that got me through it.

I went through the navy training and did well enough in flight school to become a Grumman F6F Hellcat fighter pilot. I flew combat missions from the carrier U.S.S. *Essex* and loved my work. My superiors looked on me as a well-qualified pilot, and I loved flying. I loved having control of that plane and seeing the

around in whatever the car du jour happened to be. Earl went to work for his father after high school. Over a long period of time, his family became very important to me.

I took a different path after high school, one I wasn't happy about. School never agreed with me,

and I went to college only because of my grandmother's insistence. I enrolled at Westminster College for a semester, then transferred to Washington University. (That's where the lousy grades that my brother

16

In late 1944 the Hellcat pilots of Airgroup 15, of which Jack was a member, gathered on the hangar deck of the U.S.S. Essex, above. Jack is in the back row, the seventh man from the right. The commander of Airgroup 15 was David McCampbell, one of the navy's all-time leading air aces, pictured sixth from the right in the second row. The stripe across the tail of the airplane was the identification symbol for Airgroup 15, enabling pilots to spot each other in the midst of skies that were often cloudy or crowded with planes. Many years later Jack and several of his navy buddies went to an aircraft museum in Florida, near right, to see the war birds, the planes from World War II.

Early in 1944 Jack and other pilots went through operational training in Vero Beach, Florida, above, prior to leaving for the Pacific. These pilots scattered to serve on many different carriers; only one other pilot in the photo above went with Jack to the U.S.S. Essex. In June 1944 the fighter pilots in Airgroup 15 signed dollar bills for each other, left, as mementos at Eniwetok Atoll, which was then a major refueling and rearming station.

This letter to Jack accompanied his second distinguished flying cross, awarded for his successful work against enemy fighters. A typical mission for Jack's airgroup was both a fighting and a bombing mission. Jack and his fellow pilots searched for and engaged Japanese planes in the air. They would then bomb any planes they found on the ground if they had enough fuel to continue.

THE SECRETARY OF THE NAVY
WASHINGTON

The President of the United States takes pleasure in presenting the DISTINGUISHED FLYING CROSS to

LIEUTENANT, JUNIOR GRADE, JACK CRAWFORD TAYLOR
UNITED STATES NAVAL RESERVE

for service as set forth in the following

CITATION:

"For heroism and extraordinary achievement in aerial flight as Pilot of a Plane in Fighting Squadron FIFTEEN, attached to the U.S.S. ESSEX, in action against enemy Japanese forces over Formosa, on October 12, 1944. A daring and intrepid airman carrying out a bold fighter sweep mission, Lieutenant, Junior Grade, (then Ensign) Taylor executed a vigorous attack against an overwhelming number of hostile aircraft and, skillfully maneuvering his plane, destroyed two enemy fighters and assisted his squadron in the destruction of nineteen others. By his airmanship, courage and devotion to duty, he contributed to the infliction of extensive damage upon the enemy and upheld the highest traditions of the United States Naval Service."

For the President,

James Forrestal

Secretary of the Navy

10A   St. Louis Globe-Democrat. Thurs., Dec. 14, 1944

Pilot Home From Pacific Is One of 3 St. Louisans With 'Fabled 15'

Snow-blanketed St. Louis under still-falling flakes was a most welcome sight for Ensign Jack Crawford Taylor, who came back yesterday for Christmas leave after more than seven months in South and Central Pacific areas with the "Fabled Fifteen" Air Group aboard the carrier Essex, he said on arrival yesterday at the home of his parents, Mr. and Mrs. Mel M. Taylor, 34 Oakleigh lane, Clayton.

"Three St. Louis pilots were in bomber pilot in Fifteen," Taylor continued, "but his duties required him to remain on the West Coast a little longer." Brodhead was met by his wife, the former Josephine Carr, 4387 Westminster pl., who informed her parents yesterday they would be home before Christmas. Brodhead has the Distinguished Flying Cross and Air Medal with Gold Star, in lieu of a second award, for participation in 45 combat sorties and a strike on a 30,000-ton Japanese ship of the ISE class BB, XCV, during fleet action of Oct. 24-25.

Taylor destroyed two and a half enemy craft while airborne and took part in destruction of or damage to 388 enemy planes in the air and on the ground. His group received credit for 174,300

IDENTIFICATION CARD   701 83 81

THIS IS TO CERTIFY THAT

Jack Crawford .... TAYLOR
(Name)

34 Oakleigh lane .... Clayton, Missouri
(Address)

Has enlisted as a V-5 Aviation Cadet in the United States Naval Reserve

Sept. 23, 1942
(Date)

NACSB-100

LT., A-U(S), U.S.N.R.

Fleet Officers' Club
ULITHI LAGOON

No. 1741

Jack Crawford Taylor
is a Member of this Club

Secretary-Treasurer

Jack and his Hellcat fighter, left, were a formidable part of Airgroup 15, which shot down more planes than any other group. Jack himself was headlined upon his return to St. Louis. The identification card on the left is from Jack's enlistment in the U.S.N.R. in 1942, and the card above is his membership card in the Fleet Officers' Club, Ulithi Lagoon.

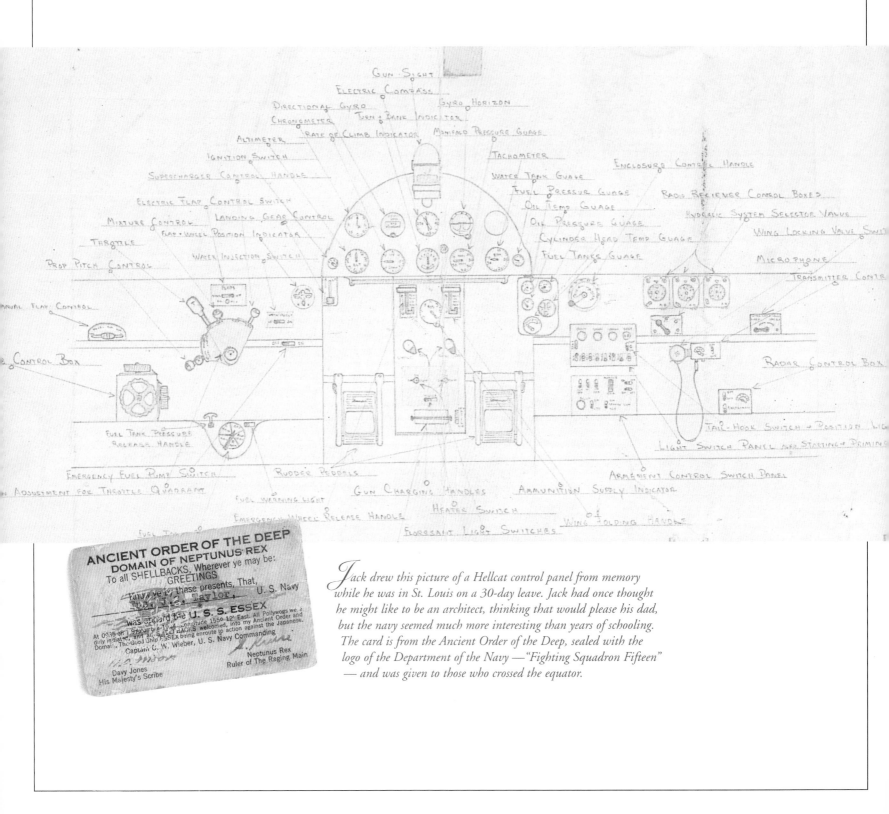

Jack drew this picture of a Hellcat control panel from memory while he was in St. Louis on a 30-day leave. Jack had once thought he might like to be an architect, thinking that would please his dad, but the navy seemed much more interesting than years of schooling. The card is from the Ancient Order of the Deep, sealed with the logo of the Department of the Navy —"Fighting Squadron Fifteen"— and was given to those who crossed the equator.

Jack and Mary Ann were married at Second Presbyterian Church in St. Louis on February 15, 1945. They pose here with their parents and three of Mary Ann's bridesmaids. It was 70 degrees that day, an unheard of phenomenon in St. Louis in the middle of winter. The next day the newlyweds left St. Louis to drive to California and soon ran into an ice storm.

world below me. Landing the plane on the deck of the aircraft carrier was a tremendous challenge, and I worked hard to perfect my skill in bringing the plane on board — I was determined to land perfectly every time, and I did. There was always a certain danger present, but by controlling specific risks, we minimized the unknown danger that was inevitably beyond our control.

As a fighter pilot in World War II, I felt I was really in my element. Flying gave me a great deal of satisfaction as a member of a team, like later when I ran a business. It was a powerful feeling to keep in touch with the men on the wingtips and to fly in formation with a bunch of buddies. That sounds like navy talk, and I guess it is. But when you're up there over the water in a simple pattern that looks like geese flying south, you are totally discon-

nected from the world below and you don't think about problems. The beauty of the teamwork is its simplicity — everybody is in the right place, the leader points the way and you all move together as one.

When MacArthur landed in the Philippines, he needed increased air support, and I continued to fly combat missions as the pace of the war in the Pacific picked up. Later, the *Essex* was sent back to port to refuel and rearm, so for about a week some other junior pilots and I were assigned to fly combat missions from the U.S.S. *Enterprise*. (Little did I know then that the name Enterprise would play an important part in my life. Years later I picked that name for the business because I liked the sound of it.)

Those years were an important time in my life for many reasons. Mary Ann MacCarthy and I had dated for five years, and we got married in 1945. I met her through my brother, Paul, while she was still in high school, and I was a couple of years older than she was. I went to St. Louis on leave in February 1945, and we got married. She and I then drove back to California, where I was stationed. After the war ended later that year, life as a pilot became much more relaxed, and we loved being in California. We had good friends there and did a lot of sailing. It was a nice life, but I knew I had to move on. I left the navy in September 1945. Mary Ann and I drove from California back to St. Louis in a Studebaker Champion that I had

19

bought from Earl Lindburg's father.

Civilian life was a very different routine, and I soon got busy looking for a job in St. Louis. I asked my dad if the stock brokerage business was a growing business. He said about six million shares were traded every day, maybe someday it would hit ten million shares a day. I wasn't impressed; it didn't look to me like the kind of fast-changing business with expanding opportunities that I was looking for. In 1945 nobody I knew had any idea that the brokerage business would turn into round-the-clock trading of stocks and bonds from all over the world, with hundreds of millions of transactions every day.

The single-engine-fighter-pilot syndrome of being in control kept bubbling up inside me, so after a brief stint with a paper company in a job that didn't really excite me, I bought a used 1937 Chevrolet panel truck and started my own delivery service in Clayton. I charged a quarter a package,

and I made deliveries to all kinds of customers, including night runs for a drug store. My instinct to be my own

Jack and Mary Ann lived at 9808 Conway Road from the time Andy was three years old until he was in the seventh grade. Jack bought the lot for $3,000 and built a house for $15,000. It was a cozy three-bedroom ranch with one-and-a-half bathrooms and one air conditioning window unit in Jack and Mary Ann's bedroom. The shadow of the photographer's head, probably Jack's, looms in the foreground while Andy and Jo Ann sit patiently in the yard.

boss was the right one to follow — in two years I had four vehicles.

By the time my son, Andy, was born in 1947, the delivery business was going well. I often put him in a laun-

dry basket on the front seat and took him on delivery runs. Andy loved to ride in the truck — maybe that's where he learned to love cars and things that go fast. I was probably a little bit compulsive about my work — regardless of the time of day or the weather, I got the deliveries out. I knew that the business would only succeed if I made it succeed. Mary Ann was always supportive — she knew that I needed a challenge in my work, and she was great with the kids, even when I had to put in long hours. Our daughter, Jo Ann, was born two years after Andy, and I felt good about the way life was treating me. I worked hard, but I felt that we were all in it together.

Somehow the word spread about my delivery business and the hard work I was putting into it. Earl Lindburg's father, Arthur, was a friend of the owner of a dress shop for whom I made deliveries, and Arthur mentioned that he wanted to hire some enthusiastic young guys to come to work in the car business. The dress shop owner told him about me — that I was a determined young man — and Arthur asked Earl to call me. Earl said his father wanted to hire me and asked if I would come to work at Lindburg Cadillac. I liked being my own boss and wasn't interested in going to work for someone else. I told him, "No, Earl. I've got this little business, and I'm making enough money. Thanks, but things are going fine for me." I didn't give his offer another thought.

Several months later Earl asked me to ride to the airport with his father. On the way Mr. Lindburg said to me, "Jack, this car business is going to be expanding, and I want some hard-working young men to come to work for me. I hear you're a pretty good worker, and I want you to work at the dealership." I told him I didn't know anything about the car business and asked what he expected me to do. He said he didn't know, he would figure out something. Then he looked me straight in the eye and made me an offer of $400 a month — $400 a month in those days was worth more than most starting salaries today. I was astounded. That was twice what I was making in my delivery business. I hadn't realized how much of an impression I

had made. I relented and told him, "Okay, Mr. Lindburg, I'll do it." That's how I got into the car business.

Learning the Business

Jack Taylor's decision to give up his own business and go to work for someone else had a dramatic and immediate impact — he went from being the man in charge to being low man on the totem pole. His willingness to give up his growing business and go to work for Arthur Lindburg was a leap of faith driven by the conviction that there would be good opportunities down the road. Jack did not ask for a job description, a listing of benefits, vacations or hours — he just said "yes" and showed up for work. In 1948, at the age of 26, he started work at Lindburg Cadillac, located on the corner of Sarah and Laclede in the midtown part of the city, with a salary of $400 a month and no notion about how the car business worked.

In his first few months, those good opportunities he had envisioned seemed very far down the road. Jack went to work in a coat and tie; he reported to a porter named Ike Keys. Instead of delivering neat and tidy packages for the shopkeepers of

Clayton, now he swept the showroom floor, put license plates on cars, made trips to the license bureau and got car documents ready for the salesmen. Although pushing a broom and screwing on license plates was far different from the life of a navy pilot, Jack adapted quickly. He liked the people he worked with, and his motivation to learn the car business kept him pushing hard and smiling.

Jack's industriousness brought rapid advancement. After a few months, Arthur Lindburg sent him to be a used car salesman at the same lot where he had purchased his first car — a Studebaker — years earlier. After selling used cars for several months, Jack became a new car salesman at Lindburg's Clayton dealership, which sold both Cadillacs and Oldsmobiles. Earl had already been moved to the Clayton dealership by his father, and the two buddies settled in to handle new car sales.

Because new cars weren't readily available during the war years, there was a huge pent-up demand for new cars when hostilities ended and car manufacturers turned from making armaments to making automobiles. Being a car salesman was more a matter of taking orders than of selling

ANDY & JO ANN 9808 CONWAY RD 1951

During the early years on Conway Road, Jack was a salesman for Lindburg Cadillac and living a comfortable but modest life. No company cars were provided, however, and in 1951 Andy and Jo Ann stood sternly in front of the family car, a four-door that Jack had purchased to accommodate the family of four.

aggressively, since cars were in short supply. Customers often had to take what they could get. During that time much of the challenge was keeping customers happy when their cars were delayed at the factory and were not delivered on schedule. Jack developed a knack for dealing with customers by giving them an honest explanation of the status of their car.

22

"Well, let me give you my best estimate on when the car will get here," was the starting point for most of his discussions with customers. When they pressed, Jack would continue: "I don't work in the factory, I don't build these cars myself, so I can't tell you with absolute certainty when it will get here. I can tell you that I will keep following up on it, and I'll let you know as soon as I know anything." These were people not easily pleased — people who wanted a car now, only to be told that it wasn't in yet. It was a matter of doing a dance and keeping the customer happy, since Jack's goal was repeat business with his customers.

Customers posed all sorts of challenges for an eager young salesman. One day, during a tight shortage of cars, a hard-bargaining man offered Jack $400 if he would sell him the first Cadillac to come in. Jack knew the $400 was equal to a month's pay, but he also knew that the Cadillac was promised to someone else. He refused the $400, and the customer left. That was not the last time he was offered money under the table, but Jack made up his mind he would never take it.

JACK MANAGES AND ARTHUR MENTORS

In the 1950s cars became more readily available, and selling became more of a challenge. Arthur Lindburg hired more salesmen, and he made Jack the sales manager in Clayton. The business continued to grow, and Arthur transferred Earl from the Clayton dealership to the downtown office and promoted Jack to

take Earl's place as manager of the entire Clayton dealership. Jack's progress had been fast — from sweeping the showroom floor to running a dealership in a few years. Arthur Lindburg liked Jack and enjoyed watching his progress in the business as much as he enjoyed watching Earl's progress. Intuition had motivated Jack's decision to take the first job with Arthur Lindburg, and it had become clear to him that hard work was the ticket to new opportunities.

The continuing expansion of the Lindburg automobile business meant that Jack was soon asked to work downtown as sales manager for the Lindburg distributorship, which was larger and more complex than a single dealership. As sales manager of the distributorship, Jack focused his attention on the retail side of the business rather than distributing wholesale cars to other dealers. He developed a large and loyal base of customers who liked doing business with him — they went away feeling good about Jack and about the way he dealt with them. He kept up the coat-and-tie routine, both for himself and for all of his salesmen, and customers liked his style.

Jack's relationship with Arthur Lindburg continued to evolve during those early years. One day, at a time when Cadillacs were readily available, Jack was talking with a customer who had a classy appearance and seemed eager to buy a car. Arthur walked through the showroom, saw them talking and motioned for Jack to come into his office. He told Jack not to sell a car to the man because he had a history of bad credit problems.

Jack went back to the customer and soon learned that the man had a check to pay for the car. Then he talked with Earl, who was at that time general manager of the distributorship and Jack's direct boss. He told Earl the customer had a check

but that Arthur had told him that the man's finances were questionable and that he was not trustworthy. Earl thought about it and said, "Sell him the car." So Jack did.

Arthur turned out to be right: the man's check was no good. Jack had to take back the car, which could no longer be sold as "new" and was now worth less money. Arthur was furious because Jack had ignored his order to turn the buyer away. Arthur decided to punish Jack by making him pay the full retail price for the car himself.

Jack explained that he had discussed Arthur's views with Earl, and that Earl, as his boss, had told

him to sell the car. With the whole story now explained, Jack offered to resign if Arthur still thought he had acted improperly. Arthur abruptly changed the subject, and it was never raised again.

Jack had learned how to disagree and sometimes argue with Arthur, but he did it in a very deferential manner. While Arthur Lindburg was still clearly the boss, the two men had established a working relationship in which each created space for the other, and neither one wanted to cause a confrontation. Jack appreciated the intellect and intuition that Arthur Lindburg invested in the business, and Arthur came to

23

Jack's first convertible was, appropriately, a dark green Cadillac with a green and white interior. The wide whitewall tires, a mark of distinction in the 1950s, were nice to look at but tough to keep clean. In the background is a 1950 Ford station wagon "woody."

FIRST CADILLAC CONVERTABLE 1955

see Jack as a creative man with deep integrity who also cared about the business.

PARTNERS WITH A NEW AMBITION

It was at the Lindburg Cadillac distributorship that Jack became interested in car leasing. Automobile leasing was nothing new, but it was not a common practice in the automobile business — just a few local leasing companies operating on a small scale. Greyhound was in the car-leasing business in Chicago and was doing a significant business leasing Cadillacs. When Greyhound started bringing leased Cadillacs that had been purchased elsewhere into the St. Louis market, suddenly potential buyers of Lindburg Cadillacs had an alternative source. The fact that Cadillacs were being brought into his territory angered Arthur Lindburg.

Arthur Lindburg saw leasing as a new, fast-growing business. He and Jack began studying the ins and outs of leasing cars in order to figure out the best way to start an automobile-leasing business. Jack studied what Greyhound was doing, he talked to others in the business and he developed the framework of a plan to start leasing cars.

While researching the leasing business, Jack realized that leasing was much more flexible and offered far more opportunities for growth than running a dealership. In the leasing business he could provide whatever car was hot at a particular time without being limited to one product line. He also realized that he could locate offices anywhere he chose without having to clear those new locations with a factory. Leasing companies could have as many locations as they wanted without having to get approval from a manufacturer. Multiple locations and a wide range of cars meant that the only limitations on the business were money and energy. He knew he had the energy and felt he could locate whatever money was necessary.

For Jack, the real allure of leasing was that leasing would be more challenging than grinding out sales of the same product line day after day — and more fun. Because leasing was more flexible, he could do a much better job of meeting the particular needs of a customer, and taking care of customers was the part of the business that he loved.

On a rainy winter afternoon in early 1957, Jack made up his mind that he was ready to begin this venture. The next day he told Arthur that he wanted to start and run a car-leasing business

for him. Arthur agreed with Jack's proposal, but told Jack he would have to wait until a replacement could be found for his current job. He also told Jack that his pay would have to be cut from $2,000 a month to $750 a month. The leasing business would not generate any income in the beginning, and Jack would have to build it into something substantial in order to be paid more money.

Jack understood the rationale but felt $750 a month was not enough. Unlike his ride to the airport when he accepted Arthur's offer with no questions, this time he negotiated his compensation, and the two of them agreed on a salary of $1,000 a month plus a bonus, both of which were to be reevaluated as the business grew. Arthur Lindburg invested $25,000 in the leasing business, Earl invested $25,000 and Earl's younger brother Clinton put in $25,000. Jack invested $10,000 (which was all he had at the time), and Arthur loaned him $15,000 so that each partner would have an equal financial investment. (Jack had planned to take out a mortgage loan on his house, but instead, Arthur Lindburg loaned Jack the $15,000 so he would not have to borrow against his house.)

Executive Leasing was the name

24

$\mathcal{S}$ETTING THE PACE

27

Jack's focus from the beginning was on getting the leasing business started as quickly as possible rather than waiting for all the details to fall into place. He loved the challenge of getting it started, and he wanted to show Arthur Lindburg that he could make it work.

Even though the office would not open for another month, the first leasing contract was signed in February 1957 by a man with whom Jack had done business at Lindburg Cadillac. Jack knew that the man was looking to buy a car for his wife, so he proposed that the man lease a car instead. After negotiating the terms of the lease, the customer agreed to the deal. Jack delivered to him a bronze-colored Chevrolet Bel Air hardtop coupe, a V-8 with automatic transmission and power steering. With the leasing of that first car, Executive Leasing was in business.

Once the decision was made to start the leasing business, the emphasis was on moving ahead as quickly as possible. Because a bookkeeping system was not yet in place, financial records were kept in the bank book. The initial deposit of capital — $40,000 — was made at the First National Bank in St. Louis in February 1957. With money in the bank and the first customer on the books, it was a great month.

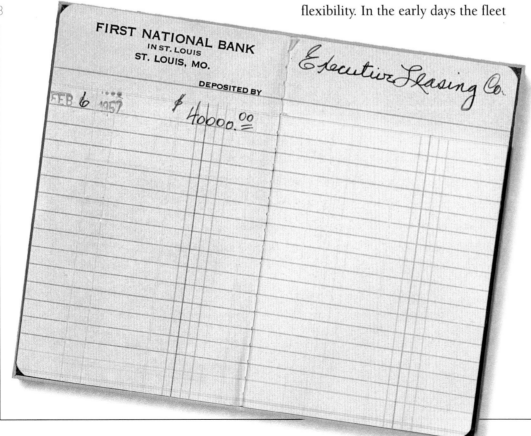

AN UPSCALE BUSINESS IN A LOWER-LEVEL LOCATION

The office of Executive Leasing that opened in March 1957 was humble and unpretentious; it was in the basement of Arthur Lindburg's Forest Cadillac dealership in Clayton next to the body shop. Through an understanding with Arthur Lindburg, the plan for Executive Leasing from the outset was to lease any make of car other than Cadillacs. That kept the retail Cadillac business strong in the Lindburg dealerships and gave Jack flexibility. In the early days the fleet consisted primarily of General Motors models, and Jack soon built a strong base of business leasing a variety of cars.

Two bays of the body shop were converted into the new leasing office by installing sheets of plywood to separate Jack and his leasing staff from the mechanics. The plywood was painted a pale green to bring some color into the basement. Perhaps the green was an unknown omen at the time, foretelling the future financial success of the company and the green of the Enterprise corporate logo. Both the financial success and the corporate logo lay far in the future, but Jack's motivation to make this business work was clear from the outset.

The entire office space was about the size of two normal bedrooms, and there were no closets. For the first several months, the entire staff was Jack and Nell Mason, who handled all the bookkeeping and administrative functions. A year after opening, Bob Mohan was hired as a salesman, and he and Jack each sat in a portion of the space that had been sectioned off with waist-high partitions. Each salesman had a chair and a metal desk with drawers on one side. There was a chair for a customer, but the space was so tight they had to ask the customer to move his

From the beginning of Executive Leasing, Jack maintained a management style of working closely and directly with his salesmen. Motivation, attention to detail and thorough follow-up were topics of frequent discussion, just as they were when Jack was sales manager at Lindburg Cadillac. Here Jack talks with the Lindburg Cadillac sales force and General Manager Earl Lindburg, center, in the dark suit, in 1955.

*I*n 1957 the carriage-trade Cadillac customers shopped for cars upstairs at Forest Cadillac, which faced Carondelet Avenue at the top of this photo. Executive Leasing's customers entered off Hanley Road, on the right in this photo. By the time this photo was taken, the business was growing and a portion of the wall was knocked down to make a new entrance at the back of the building so that customers could walk directly from the parking lot into the basement office. The auto show in St. Louis, left, was a big event each year, with entertainment, food and drink in addition to the new cars. These new 1958 Cadillacs were being sold upstairs at the Forest dealership while Jack and his team were leasing Bel Airs and other models downstairs.

legs in order to open the desk drawer. After a year or so the administrative staff was increased to four women, two of whom sat at each end of the office space with Jack and Bob Mohan in the middle.

They were cramped quarters, but it was the pneumatic tools from the body shop that created the biggest problem. When the tools started to whine and clatter, the plywood walls hardly dampened the sound at all and nobody could hear on the telephone. Everybody — including customers on the other end of the line — had to wait until the tools stopped.

It was an unusual scene in the lower-level office, with salesmen often shouting into the phone in order to be heard over the surrounding din and administrative helpers passing paperwork rapidly back and forth while the salesmen negotiated deals. It looked more like a stockbrokers' trading room in the 1990s than an automobile leasing office in the 1950s. The pace was often hectic, phones rang constantly and

everybody in the office focused on one thing — close the deal, get the lease done. It was a closely knit team in which everyone knew his or her own role but also picked up the slack whenever necessary. Everybody answered phones, calculated lease rates, filled out paperwork and took care of customers.

With the entire staff of sales and administrative people squeezed into

Executive Leasing's first location, in the lower level of the Forest Cadillac building, was a much less impressive place than the Lindburg Cadillac building illustrated above, where Jack had been sales manager. This grand building, located near downtown St. Louis, later became the third Executive Leasing office. It was also the spot Arthur Lindburg selected for his office. That way he could keep an eye on both Cadillac sales and Executive Leasing's activities.

this subterranean space, Executive Leasing was under way. Forest Cadillac at Hanley Road and Carondelet Avenue was a well-regarded location, and Jack described his company as being in the "lower level" of the dealership rather than in the basement. His clientele was an affluent crowd; many were Cadillac customers he had known. Jack wanted the leasing business to make a pleasant and efficient impression, at least as much as was possible given the physical circumstances of their surroundings.

Though he could not change the appearance of the basement, he could decide what appearance he and his people would present. "I wanted my people to look like bankers," Jack says in describing how he felt about personal appearance. "If they looked like bankers, they would clearly differentiate themselves from salesmen in other car businesses." With that look of professionalism also came respect from customers, and that was crucial in building the leasing business at a time when leasing a personal car was not the conventional pattern.

That look of first-rate professionalism was applicable to everyone, whether they were visible to customers or in the back. Early on a new man was hired to work in the service department of Executive Leasing. He arrived with slicked-back long hair, long sideburns, black leather boots, and black leather pants and jacket. Though he was glad to get a new man, when Jack first saw him, he said, "You lose the hair, you lose the black leather and the boots, and you're on." The next morning the new employee came in nicely shaved, wearing jeans and a plain shirt. He kept the job.

In the early days at Forest Cadillac, Bob Mohan was one of the people who set the style for the business. Mohan worked for the then-called *St. Louis Globe-Democrat* selling advertising to car dealerships when Jack first met him. He was bright, quick and charming, and Jack found him fun to work with. Prior to selling advertising, Mohan had sold shoes at Famous-Barr department store, and it was clear to Jack that he had the sales instinct in his blood. When Jack offered him a job, Mohan was concerned about being able to communicate effectively with Cadillac customers — he felt they might be different from customers he had known who bought newspaper ads or shoes in a department store.

Jack took Mohan to Brooks Brothers and got him out of polyester and into the "right" look. Mohan responded to Jack's tutelage and thrived as a salesman. His persistence with the customers in closing deals was legendary, and his flamboyant style brought levity to the office whenever the pace seemed overbearing.

One day Mohan was trying to complete a lease for a very proper older lady who was satisfied with the terms of the deal but concerned about the white interior of the car. "Ma'am, people who roll around in ash pits might have a problem with this interior, but with the way you live and the places that you go, I don't think you have a worry in the world." The lady smiled and the deal was done.

FACE-TO-FACE LEADERSHIP

It was a combination of Jack's leadership and the cramped quarters that forged these people into a closely knit team. Though each salesman worked on a commission basis, they concentrated from the beginning on taking care of customers, and teamwork took the place of arguing over commissions. Because they all sat very close together, they overheard conversations and knew what everyone else was doing. This gave them the knowledge to cover for each other when needed, and everybody

32

The REALITIES
of a Family Business

Jack and Mary Ann were also busy raising a family in Executive Leasing's early days. Jack came home for family dinner every night and talked about the business with Mary Ann and their two kids, Andy and Jo Ann. Mary Ann watched over their education, and Jack encouraged Andy when he played football and Jo Ann as she played field hockey. School, sports and business were the usual dinner-time topics, and family and business became comfortably intertwined.

From the earliest days of the business, Mary Ann went on countless repossession ventures with Jack to bring back cars from customers who had not made their lease payments. Jack tracked down cars to be repossessed, and then Mary Ann would drive out with him to bring one back. (Leasing companies, like lenders who finance car purchases, move quickly when customers fail to make payments. They repossess the car as fast as possible in order to resell it before its value declines and therefore avoid taking a loss.)

One Saturday morning Jack and Mary Ann took a car out of a garage that was situated under the house of the customer. The customer was upstairs in the house playing the piano while Jack tried to get the right key to start the car. He knew that he was safe as long as he could hear her playing the piano. He worked fast, and he and Mary Ann drove safely away while the soon-to-be-surprised leasing customer happily played tune after tune on her piano. This husband and wife repo team was the first of many in Enterprise's history.

Notwithstanding the demands of a fast-growing business, Jack and Mary Ann took family vacations every year. Jack had grown up taking trips with his parents and grandparents, and he and Mary Ann wanted Andy and Jo Ann to travel and to have fun together as a family. The 1960 vacation was to Jackson Hole, Wyoming, and included a ski-lift ride for Jack and Jo Ann.

PASSING ON
the Taylor Philosophy

Jack's hard work — and his enthusiasm — were evident to Andy and Jo Ann. They watched him work at the kitchen table with his calculator when it was time to put together new leasing rates, and they often shared his Saturday morning trips to the office.

As a young boy, Andy did not know what a lease was, but he was proud of his dad because he knew he worked hard and liked what he was doing. Jack began talking with Andy about some of the practical realities of running a fledgling business: "You know that we're starting this new business, and I want you to take care of your school khakis. When you play ball after school, you slide around and ruin your good pants. I'd rather have you put on your old jeans to go out and play ball because we won't have as much money until we get this business going."

Years later, when money was not a problem, Andy regularly splurged on khakis and kept a huge supply in his closet — a simple way to balance the score from times past.

The decade of the 1950s was the height of car culture. With tail fins and gleaming chrome, cars represented personal style, taste and affluent living. Most of all, cars represented a new type of freedom that changed nearly every aspect of daily life.

learned different parts of the business.

By 1959 the entire staff consisted of seven people nestled in one basement room that was bursting at its plywood seams. The leasing business grew steadily, and as it grew the business and accounting functions required more detailed attention. In the spring of 1959 Ruby Garrison was hired to handle much of the administrative work in the office. She had young children at the time and initially only worked until three in the afternoon. One filing cabinet held all the customer files, all the insurance files and the paid bills. Nell Mason was in charge of accounting, and she kept the checkbook in her desk drawer. Though many of the administrative procedures were informal, they were carefully divided, and Jack made sure that they were closely followed. The administra-

tive requirements grew quickly as the number of leases increased. Ruby Garrison soon was working full time, and every time she needed a new filing cabinet, the office space got a little more cramped.

The friendship and the fun that were part of the daily routine in the late 1950s became an essential part of how the company operated. Managers were accessible, people knew what others were doing and how they were doing, and the overriding sense of teamwork bound them together. When it came time to hire another salesman, they knocked out a plywood wall and took over more space from the body shop. Bob Mohan kept the crowd laughing, and when work was over, they often went for a drink, more often than not to talk about the day's experiences. Laughter was an effective

*W*hether they were filling up for the morning commute, above, or unpacking a weekend barbecue, right, people needed cars that fit their needs. Leasing and rental were flexible options for many drivers, and Executive Leasing worked to broaden its leasing and rental fleets to accommodate both the weekend trip and the daily grind.

The Hiring
PROCESS

Mike Schwarz graduated from high school in 1959, and he thought briefly about following in his father's footsteps as a carpenter. After a few months pounding nails, he quickly realized that his love of cars had more long-term potential than nailing roofing on houses in the blazing heat of August. A high school friend told Schwarz that Executive Leasing was beginning to hire people, and he jumped at the opportunity.

Schwarz was hired after one interview with the operations manager because his enthusiasm was apparent even though his experience was limited. Like many others, Schwarz was hired because of his eagerness and his determination, and his attention to detail paid off on the job. His job was to take care of the growing fleet of cars, preparing them for customers and having them in the right place at the right time for the salesmen. He worked hard, and over a number of years Schwarz became a critical link in the dealer relationships as the need for cars continued to expand and the purchasing and movement of cars became increasingly important in assuring high-quality customer service.

Uncle Sam called Schwarz into the army during the Vietnam war, and for 18 months he was away from the company. After that stint he was welcomed back into his prior position, a position that had grown considerably during his absence since there were now many more cars in the fleet.

Though initial customers came through the Cadillac

The beginnings of the leasing business were built primarily on word-of-mouth marketing with limited newspaper ads. Customer service was thus the company's greatest promotional tool. By the time the business expanded into rental some years later, newspaper ads, below and opposite, were a regular part of the marketing effort to bring in new business, but quality service was still what brought the customers back.

OUT-OF-TOWN GUESTS ARRIVING For CHRISTMAS? ․․․․․ Rent An *Executive* Car! BY THE DAY or WEEK

COMPACT CARS AS LOW AS ․․․

$5.00 PER DAY ․․․OR․․․ $32.50 PER WEEK

PLUS 5c A MILE

• Full Size Cars—Slightly More
• Above rates include everything but gasoline

FOR INFORMATION—CALL NOW!

Executive LEASING CO. ALL MAKES AND MODELS

111 S. HANLEY CLAYTON VO. 3-0055
4927 SOUTH KINGSHIGHWAY VE. 2-8800

LINDBURG'S LEASING DIVISION

1963

GLOBE PROOFS

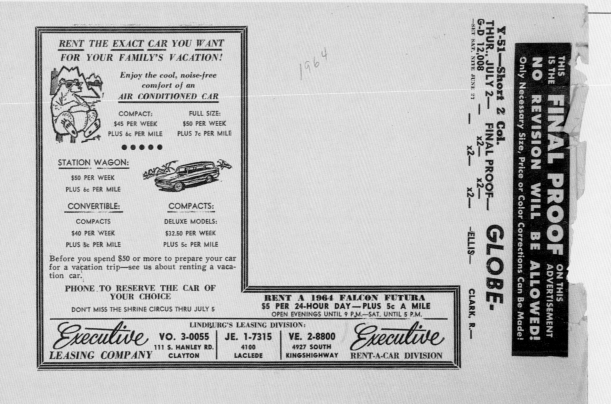

1964

Y-51—Short 2 Col.
THUR., JULY 2—
G-D 12,008 FINAL PROOF— **GLOBE-**
—SET SAT. NITE JUNE 27

—x2— —x2— —x2— —ELLIS— CLARK, R—

RENT THE EXACT CAR YOU WANT FOR YOUR FAMILY'S VACATION!

Enjoy the cool, noise-free comfort of an **AIR CONDITIONED CAR**

COMPACT: $45 PER WEEK PLUS 6¢ PER MILE

FULL SIZE: $50 PER WEEK PLUS 7¢ PER MILE

STATION WAGON:
$50 PER WEEK
PLUS 6¢ PER MILE

CONVERTIBLE:
COMPACTS
$40 PER WEEK
PLUS 8¢ PER MILE

COMPACTS:
DELUXE MODELS:
$32.50 PER WEEK
PLUS 5¢ PER MILE

Before you spend $50 or more to prepare your car for a vacation trip—see us about renting a vacation car.

PHONE TO RESERVE THE CAR OF YOUR CHOICE

DON'T MISS THE SHRINE CIRCUS THRU JULY 5

RENT A 1964 FALCON FUTURA
$5 PER 24-HOUR DAY — PLUS 5¢ A MILE
OPEN EVENINGS UNTIL 9 P.M.—SAT. UNTIL 5 P.M.

LINDBURG'S LEASING DIVISION:

Executive
LEASING COMPANY

VO. 3-0055
111 S. HANLEY RD.
CLAYTON

JE. 1-7315
4100
LACLEDE

VE. 2-8800
4927 SOUTH
KINGSHIGHWAY

Executive
RENT-A-CAR DIVISION

---

dealership, word of mouth worked well to advertise the new business. Executive Leasing did use print advertising, appearing regularly in the lower left corner of the sports page of the *St. Louis Post-Dispatch*. Even with this broader advertising, the customer base remained a silk-stocking trade, and there was a heavy preponderance of high-end American cars in the leasing fleet.

As the company's reputation for quality service grew, both the customer base and the fleet became more diverse.

Jack could get any type of car, thus fitting a customer's particular need better than a dealer with a limited line of products. Jack knew pride of ownership was an important motivator in the purchase of a new car. Although the cars were in fact owned by the leasing company, Jack emphasized that each car was "the customer's car." Pride of ownership became as commonplace with these leased cars as with cars that consumers bought and owned directly.

FIRST PROOF

Rent A 1964 Compact Car
FROM
Executive
LEASING COMPANY
For As Little As
$5 Per Day
Plus
5¢ Per Mile!
Please Call
VO 3-0055
CLAYTON
VE 2-8800
SOUTH

medicine that took the edge off intense daily routines.

FORGING A NEW PHILOSOPHY

Arthur Lindburg's philosophy about the car business guided the early evolution of Executive Leasing. Lindburg had watched many of his competitors regularly engage in practices that demeaned their customers. While such tactics generated a few more dollars of short-term revenue for the dealers, they clearly jeopardized long-term customer relationships and profitability. Hard-sell tactics were commonplace in the industry.

Some customers learned that the car they ultimately purchased was not the one they had looked at or taken for a test drive. "Read the serial number. That's the one you got," was the salesman's reply, a response that left little or no recourse for a disgruntled customer. When it came time for servicing, warranties were often treated with little respect by some dealers who took full advantage of the classic seller's market.

Many automobile dealers during the 1950s and 1960s not only practiced questionable sales tactics, but they also were mere faultfinders when presented with problems. They frequently pointed fingers and found fault with others rather than asking themselves, "What can we do to fix it?" If they had a factory problem, they got mad at the factory. If they had a customer problem, the customer bore the brunt of it. All too often their goal was volume and market share, with little attention to long-term viability and profitability.

During the 1940s the car manufacturers had relied on their network of fiercely independent dealers to handle all aspects of both sales and service of automobiles. Just as sales techniques varied among the dealers, attention to customer service was also left up to individual dealers and was not controlled by the manufacturers. After World War II there was a huge pent-up demand for cars, and the manufacturers were more concerned about delivering cars than about providing high-quality customer service. Even when the manufacturers were aware that inferior customer service was being provided by a dealer, they rarely intervened. This manufacturer-dealer relationship resulted in a very fragmented system of customer service that was prevalent in the late 1940s and continued in the 1950s. It was in that environment that Jack Taylor's philosophy about consistent, high-quality customer service had its origins, and his philosophy differentiated his business from that of his competitors.

Jack Taylor agreed with Lindburg's view that attention should be directed toward long-term strategies for doing business. At Executive Leasing any problem that surfaced called for a long-range solution. Jack was adamant about seeking solutions that would work not only at the moment, but also a month, a year or five years down the road.

Fixing rather than patching problems ran distinctly counter to the shortsighted approach of many of Executive Leasing's competitors. Automobile dealers were generally individual entrepreneurs who had grown up in the business as salesmen, people with a natural inclination toward transactions rather than long-lasting relationships. Jack carved out a niche for Executive Leasing in this environment — a niche that would propel the company to the top of the rental industry many years later. His determination to treat customers fairly and to differentiate his business from the competitive environment in which he worked became the early hallmark of the company.

Building a Reputation

Jack Taylor viewed Executive Leasing as a service business — a business in which uncompromising customer service was a more important investment than the cars themselves. He was adamant that his people treat every customer as they would like to be treated, and he knew that this practice would lead to long-term benefits. He operated on the basis that growth and profitability would both follow if primary attention was directed toward the customer. His fervent belief was that long-term customer loyalty could best be developed by creating a pleasant business experience that people would remember with satisfaction and share with their friends. If people felt good, they would come back, and that was the quickest way to build a solid base of business.

From the beginning Jack hired energetic people who were often young or short on experience but adept at dealing with people. He hired people who had never been in the car business, and he taught them to treat customers like intelligent men and women. People leased cars because they thought leasing was a good deal, and they did business with Executive Leasing because they liked the way Jack's people treated them. The Executive Leasing salespeople were conscientious and charming, and from the beginning they learned to look the customer in the eye and say, "Thank you."

Building Relationships

Jack valued not only his customers, but also his business associates. Although the Taylor approach to customer service differed from the pattern of many automobile dealers, Jack took care from the outset to develop close business relationships between Executive Leasing and dealers. Executive bought cars from a number of dealers in St. Louis, and since the leasing of individual cars was not commonplace and was not widely understood, Executive was perceived as something of a maverick. Dealers at that time had a definite retail focus, and they failed to see that they should offer benefits to a leasing company like Executive that bought large quantities of cars. Executive kept looking for dealers who understood the dynamics of the leasing business and built strong, long-term relationships with those dealers.

From the outset Executive stuck with the dealer relationships that worked well. Mike Schwarz developed close relationships with dealers, and many of those relationships have continued for decades. The foundation of trust and respect that Executive built laid a basis for the future growth of the dealer relationships with Enterprise. Years later many of those dealerships came to recognize the advantages of letting Enterprise handle the daily rental business of providing rental cars to the customers servicing their cars at the dealership. Today there are Enterprise rental offices on the premises of many new car dealerships, a practice that no one anticipated in 1957.

Executive was a pioneer in its industry, acting as an advocate for the customer rather than as an adversary. The company was built gradually, customer by customer, with heavy emphasis on building relationships and generating both repeat business and word-of-mouth referrals. Over the years the automobile dealers moved toward more customer-friendly practices. By the time this change occurred, Enterprise was well established and well ahead of competitors. Flying in the face of convention in the automobile business in the 1950s paid off handsomely.

The ENTERPRISE
Mission

"*Our* **mission** *is to fulfill the automobile rental, leasing, car sale, and related needs of our customers, and, in doing so,* **exceed** *their expectations for* **service, quality, and value.** ∎ *We will strive to* **earn** *our customers' long-term* **loyalty** *by working to deliver more than promised; being honest and fair, and* **'going the extra mile'** *to provide exceptional personalized service that creates a* **pleasing** *business experience.* ∎ *We must* **motivate** *our employees to provide exceptional service to our customers by* **supporting** *their development,* **providing** *opportunities for personal growth, and amply* **compensating** *them for their successes and achievements. We believe it is crucial to our success to* **promote** *managers from within who will serve as* **examples** *of success for others to follow.* ∎ *Although* **our goal is to be the best** *and not necessarily the biggest or the most profitable, our success at* **satisfying customers** *and* **motivating employees** *will bring growth and long-term profitability.*"

$\mathcal{E}$NTERING NEW MARKETS

41

In the early 1960s the leasing business continued to grow at a steady rate and was clearly the business Jack wanted to pursue. The management style of fair treatment of customers and employees and attention to long-term customer relationships had taken hold. Though there was no official mission statement in those days, the management practices that were evolving would eventually be articulated years later in Enterprise's statement of its corporate mission.

The foundation of Jack's management style was clear: treat people right and the business will thrive. When the corporate mission statement was eventually translated from an oral tradition to a written document in the early 1990s, it concluded, "our success at satisfying customers and motivating employees will bring growth and long-term profitability."

42

Even before the leasing business was showing much profit, Arthur Lindburg had pressed Jack to expand into a new location. Jack was reluctant but eventually felt that Executive could branch out of its one office without too much risk. To minimize the risk associated with opening a new location, a great deal of thought went into the selection of the location and the choice of an experienced manager to run it. It was important that it work right in the long term, not just be a quick, short-term effort.

The new location opened in 1961 on a strip of South Kingshighway known as "dealership row." The South Kingshighway office opened as a leasing office with a clear focus. The hope was that the proximity of car dealerships would bring in customers and create a demand for leasing similar to his experience in Clayton.

The most significant difference between the South Kingshighway office and the Forest Cadillac office was the customers, not the location. The people who lived in the South Kingshighway area were not as affluent as the people in Clayton. Jack respected their values and their financial conservatism — they were people who worked hard and met their financial obligations.

The new office on South Kingshighway was significant because it represented a big step forward — for the first time, Executive Leasing was on the move and out of the basement.

But of even greater importance was the movement toward a new and different type of customer. No longer were all the leasing customers of the silk-stocking variety; it was now clear that leasing was equally applicable to a much wider group of people.

With the move to South Kingshighway, the company began to grow toward the vast group of middle-income people who populate large and small cities around the country, people who would eventually become the solid core of the Enterprise customer base throughout the country. Executive Leasing was becoming a company equally at home in the limited confines of a Cadillac dealership and on Main Street, U.S.A.

The expansion effort paid off.

The leasing business grew steadily in the new office, and the South Kingshighway office would soon become a full-service location, providing rentals and used car sales in addition to leasing.

GOING DOWNTOWN

After the success of the South Kingshighway office, Arthur Lindburg and Jack discussed the possibility of Executive opening an office in downtown St. Louis. The first time around Jack had initially resisted expansion, wanting to see a steadier profit before opening the South Kingshighway location. But this time Arthur Lindburg was adamant.

"If you don't open a leasing office downtown, I will," he told Jack. It was

Automobile dealers have always tended to locate themselves close to each other. "Dealership row," a phrase known across the country, identified the place to go to do comparison shopping when buying or leasing a car. Executive Leasing's first expansion was to the St. Louis location where other car dealers were clustered, South Kingshighway, top. By the time of this photograph in 1968, the original oval logo had been replaced by the now familiar sign of the "e." A closer view of the office, above, reveals that the three elements of Enterprise's business — leasing, rental and used car sales — were already in place.

Don Ross was one of the keys to the earliest expansion of Executive Leasing. The problems he and other early managers like Doug Brown encountered would be the proving ground for the company's expansion strategy. The midtown office, seen from Market Street below, was the company's first office in downtown St. Louis and the location where Don started his career with Enterprise.

clear to Lindburg that the leasing business was growing, and he wanted to be a major player in its growth. His instincts were right, and his conversation with Jack made clear that he knew he was right. After hearing Arthur's reasoning, Jack decided to open a downtown leasing office.

Jack chose Doug Brown to open the leasing office in downtown St. Louis — the third Executive Leasing office in St. Louis. Shortly thereafter Don Ross, another one of Jack's energetic recruits, joined Doug Brown downtown. When the team of Doug Brown and Don Ross, both in their very early 20s, started building busi-

ness downtown, there was no clear-cut business plan to follow. It was up to the two of them to figure out how to generate solid leasing business. A few cars were made available for daily rentals, but they were only for customers coming in for service or maintenance. (Several years later daily rentals would become a line of business separate and distinct from leasing.) Jack was frequently around, but his role was more one of asking questions than of giving instructions.

The downtown office was almost entirely a leasing office, with only a few rental cars for special customers who needed an extra car from time to time. Though the initial motivation for opening downtown was Arthur

▲ VOlunteer 3-0055 ▲ 111 S. HANLEY ROAD ▲ CLAYTON, MISSOURI 63105

RENT-A-CAR DIVISION

March 1, 1964

	DAILY	WEEKLY	MONTHLY
COMPACTS—Corvair Monza, Rambler American Plymouth Valiant, Dodge Dart (w/ Automatic Transmission, Radio, Heater)	$5.00 plus 5¢/mile	$32.50 plus 5¢/mile	$127.50 plus 5¢/mile
MEDIUMS—Chevy II Nova, Comet Custom, Rambler Classic (w/ Automatic Transmission, Radio, Heater, Power Steering on Rambler Classic)	$6.00 plus 5¢/mile	$35.00 plus 5¢/mile	$137.50 plus 5¢mile
FULL SIZE—Chevrolet Impala, Ford Galaxie 500, Dodge Polara, Plymouth Fury (w/ Automatic Transmission, Power Steering, Power Brakes, Radio, Heater)	$7.00 plus 5¢/mile	$40.00 plus 5¢/mile	$147.50 plus 5¢/mile

GASOLINE IS NOT INCLUDED IN ABOVE RATES–RENTER FURNISHES OWN GASOLINE.

AIR CONDITIONING—In season air conditioning is available in full size cars only, at the following additional charges.	$2.00 plus 2¢/mile	$10.00 plus 2¢/mile	$25.00 plus 2¢/mile

We have two locations open to serve you:

CLAYTON
111 S. Hanley Road
Clayton, Mo. 63105
Phone: VO 3-0055

SOUTH
4927 S. Kingshighway
St. Louis, Mo. 63109
Phone: VE 2-8800

Our offices are open daily – 8:00 AM to 6:00 PM, and Saturdays – 9:00 AM to 12:30 PM.

PLEASE CALL
Donald R. Holtzmann
Daily Rental Manager
VOlunteer 3-0055

DOUG BROWN:
From Trainee to Mentor

Jack's knack for hiring the right people at the right time kept the company full of the enterprising individuals he felt were crucial for success. He was more interested in hiring people who were energetic, motivated and fun than in seeking out people primarily focused on intellectual pursuits. This hiring philosophy resulted in a relatively inexperienced staff that learned the business from Jack's point of view.

Doug Brown was 20 years old and was a married, full-time day student at St. Louis University when Brown's father introduced him to Clint Lindburg, one of Jack's partners in the newly formed Executive Leasing Company. Brown was looking for a job, and he went to see Clint Lindburg about possible employment. Though Lindburg decided not to hire Brown, he sent him downstairs to meet Jack Taylor.

Doug Brown was the 13th employee hired by Executive Leasing. Like others on the early team of Executive Leasing, Brown was brimming over with enthusiasm, a characteristic that overshadowed his experience. His job was to work as the number-one assistant in the traffic department. Brown screwed on license plates and moved cars wherever they were needed. Throughout the years many Enterprise managers would start their careers the same way Doug Brown started his.

Doug Brown was a quick study and learned the business fast. He thrived in the face of a competitive challenge. Over the years his knowledge and his insight became critical as expansion efforts took the company out of town and into new markets. He watched over the development of many inexperienced managers as they built their parts of the business, just as Jack had initially watched over him. Thus the Jack Taylor business philosophy was passed down to new generations of employees.

Following the initial success of the South Kingshighway office came the new location in midtown St. Louis on Market Street. Jack had agonized over the risks of expansion, wondering if there was a customer base downtown to support the new office and if his salesmen could perform consistently to the standard he set. Doug Brown, above, was chosen to open and manage the new "midtown" office. Don Ross joined Doug and ran the rental department.

Lindburg's insistence, it was clear to Jack that this office could reach a new group of customers. Clayton and South Kingshighway each focused on their local communities (a marketing strategy that would eventually become a fundamental part of how Enterprise does business). The objective of each office was to generate as much business as possible within an easily accessible range. Jack knew that many people worked and shopped downtown, and having a leasing office downtown would attract customers disinclined to go out of their way to do business in Clayton or on South Kingshighway.

As Executive Leasing expanded, Arthur Lindburg's role in its development began to change. Arthur kept an office in the downtown location, and he stopped by there almost every day. But with the passing of time, Arthur counted on Jack to manage the business. Even as he deferred more managerial prerogatives to Jack, Arthur continued to watch closely over Doug Brown and tell him how to run various details of the business. Brown listened, and many days he simply nodded to avoid confrontation. Other days he argued with Arthur about aspects of the leasing business that were now less understood by Arthur than by Jack's

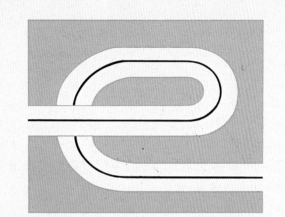

NEED A LOANER?

$6. PER DAY

EXECUTIVE RENT-A-CAR

6¢ PER MILE

CLAYTON	MIDTOWN	SOUTH
8844 LADUE RD.	2320 MARKET ST.	4927 S. KINGSHIGHWAY
VO·3·0055	CE·1·4440	VE·2·8800

During the 1960s Executive Leasing was feeling a modest amount of early success with its three locations. Midtown's leasing business continued to grow, and gradually Executive built its rental business on the tradition of dealers providing "loaners" while the customers' cars were in the shop. By the time this sign was posted, the first rental rates had been increased one dollar — now they were $6 a day and six cents a mile — and the rental business had expanded to all three Executive locations. In the early days the leasing logo was green and the rental logo was gold in order to differentiate the cars.

people in the field.

By the end of 1961 the leasing fleet had passed 1,000 cars, and with three offices, the presence of Executive Leasing was becoming more widespread throughout St. Louis. Jack went home from work one night and reported to Mary Ann the "good news" about an automobile accident on Hanley Road — for the first time, two Executive Leasing cars had collided. While it was certainly good news that no one was badly hurt, it was also good news that for the first time there were enough Executive Leasing cars around town that one had literally bumped into another.

EXPANDING THE BUSINESS:
DAILY RENTALS

In 1962 Executive Leasing entered the daily rental business, not because of a brilliant strategic insight, but because Jack gradually began to think about the ways in which a car rental business might dovetail with leasing. The more Jack thought about the rental business, the more he saw it as an additional way to provide top-quality customer service to leasing customers and as a way to generate additional income. Executive Leasing's customer base was growing

steadily, and it seemed to Jack that rentals could help solidify leasing relationships in a profitable way. He felt that if he controlled the risk by limiting the number of cars available for rental, he could test the water and see if it worked. Jack did not at that time believe that daily rentals had a huge potential, but he did see the rental business as a nice adjunct to leasing.

One Friday afternoon Jack told Don Holtzmann, who worked in the shop in the lower level of Forest Cadillac, that if Holtzmann would figure out how many cars would be needed to start a rental operation, Jack would seriously consider the idea. The following Monday morning Holtzmann came to work early, eager to talk to Jack about rentals.

"We need 17 cars to get started," Holtzmann told Jack. He never explained how he calculated that number, and Jack did not ask. The risk seemed reasonable — if it went wrong, how bad could it be, Jack thought.

"Go to it," he told Holtzmann. "See what you can do with this rental business."

Holtzmann was thrilled. He talked to every leasing customer who came in and told them that he would be glad to rent them a car anytime. Just as he had

been persistent with Jack, he was persistent in looking for rental customers, determined to prove that his idea was workable. A first step was to hire Wayne Kaufman as the first full-time rental employee of the company. Kaufman would become the driving force behind much of the expansion of the rental business. By the time he retired 30 years later as senior vice president, the rental business was the cornerstone of the company.

The initial rental business focused on replacement cars for people who needed a car for a few days. Most of the first rental cars were two-door and four-door Chevrolets, and there was an extra charge in the summer for cars with air conditioning. The basic rate was $5 a day and five cents a mile. Gradually a customer base of repeat rental customers began to grow as the story spread that you didn't have to drive to the airport to rent a car. Executive Leasing was now offering rentals at its Clayton office.

A MARKETING NICHE FOR RENTAL CARS

In the early 1960s there was no systematic marketing effort for the daily rental business. Most customers came in because they were current leasing customers or because they had heard about these rentals by word of mouth. Occasionally the Executive Leasing and Lindburg Cadillac ads on the sports page of the newspaper would mention rentals, but it was clearly a low-profile business.

By the mid-1960s, however, there was growing demand among existing leasing customers for short-term rental cars. As the rental fleet began to grow, Holtzmann and his people made a more concerted effort to generate new customers from the local area around the Clayton office. They went into nearby office buildings, wrote down the names of the businesses located there and then sent them mailers about Executive Leasing's car rental business. There was little face-to-face marketing, because the potential for the rental business was still not clear, and direct personal calls on potential customers still focused on the core business of leasing cars.

About this time, automobile insurance companies began to accept some responsibility for providing substitute transportation while their insureds' and claimants'

cars were being repaired. After losing critical court cases, the insurance companies began to pay for their customers' loss of use of their own cars after accidents by providing rental cars. The automobile replacement market suddenly blossomed in a way no one could have anticipated.

As Executive Leasing began to develop relationships with the insurance companies, the daily rental business expanded from the Clayton office to the downtown office. Doug Brown and Don Ross had started with a rental fleet of seven cars at the downtown office and felt like they were spinning their wheels finding ways to keep them rented. Brown and Ross decided to stop by an insurance office to ask if they would consider providing a temporary car to their policyholders whose cars had been stolen rather than just giving them reimbursement money. The initial response was lukewarm: "Your rate is $5 a day and a nickel a mile. Our policy only gives the $5, not the nickel." The insurance agent was not inclined to do anything differently, and Brown and Ross quickly agreed to forget the

The PARTNERSHIP

In the early 1960s Clint Lindburg decided that he did not need to continue as an investor in Executive Leasing — "I have other things to do," he told Earl and Jack. Arthur decided that it was time for the other partners to buy back Clint's share, so Clint was paid just over $100,000 for his original investment of $25,000.

Now there were three in the partnership — the father (Arthur), the son (Earl), and the operator (Jack). Shortly thereafter Arthur Lindburg, then in his middle 60s, got serious throat cancer and had his voice box removed. The prospect of his own mortality caused Arthur to think about the disposition of his one-third interest in the company. (Arthur lived to be 87, and his raspy voice and somewhat kinder nature were noticeable changes in his demeanor after he won his bout with cancer.)

As a tribute to his long-standing relationship with Jack, Arthur gave Jack one-third of his ownership share, and he

then gave the remaining two-thirds of his share to Earl. That gift — coupled with the fact that Arthur also paid the gift tax for the transfer of the stock to Jack and Earl — was an extremely generous act.

After that transaction, Jack owned 42 percent of the company and Earl owned 58 percent. This arrangement continued until the early 1970s, when a difference of opinion occurred with Arthur regarding a corporate finance matter. (Though Arthur no longer owned stock of Executive Leasing, he provided some financing for the company, so he continued to be a force to be reckoned with.) The resolution of the disagreement was that the company bought back part of Earl's stock.

After that repurchase of stock, Jack owned 75 percent of the company and Earl owned 25 percent, a comfortable arrangement for both Jack and Earl that continued for the remainder of Earl's life. At the time of Earl's death in 1986, the company retired the remainder of Earl's stock.

*L*adue Road became the headquarters for the fledgling business when it outgrew its space in the basement of Forest Cadillac. The Forest Cadillac sales office and the Carondelet Avenue administrative office were consolidated on eastern Ladue Road adjacent to Clayton on this piece of prime real estate, which remains an Enterprise location today.

nickel a mile if they could bill the insurance company directly and not have to worry about the credit of the driver. In short order all seven cars were busy all the time, and the downtown rental fleet began to grow.

The timing was perfect. Jack Taylor had already made his first foray into the local rental market, and his first taste of the business was good. He was convinced that the local daily rental business was better for him than the intensely competitive and high-cost airport rental business. He knew that his approach to superior customer service would be difficult to deliver behind an airport rental counter

where price was the major factor in the customer's mind. By the time the potential for the insurance replacement business started to become apparent, the company had already begun to capitalize on the opportunity. Times were changing in the replacement rental business, and that initial fleet of 17 rental cars had been a tiny but timely beginning.

Used Cars and the Fixed-Price System

In the early days of Executive Leasing, Ray Covington managed the resale of cars that were returned

at the end of their leases. At that time most of the cars coming back to the company at the end of leases were sold to large, wholesale used-car distributors. Other purchasers of these cars were individual dealerships, which reconditioned and then resold the cars.

With a steadily increasing volume of cars coming off lease to be sold, Executive began to outgrow these outlets — Executive was generating more cars than these wholesale buyers could readily absorb. With so many cars to sell, Ray Covington was unable to bargain effectively. As a result, the company was losing some of the

Wayne Kaufman, at left in this photo, and Ray "Whitey" Covington, at right, were two of Executive's biggest assets as the company expanded. Wayne was the first employee hired to work full time in the rental business, which he nurtured for 30 years. Ray's experience in handling the used cars generated by the leasing and rental operations made him invaluable.

potential profit of leasing since profit could only be achieved when the car was sold for a decent price at the end of the lease. It was in this environment that Jack decided to enter the retail used car business, knowing that many of Executive's own leasing customers had expressed interest in buying a good-quality used car.

The South Kingshighway location on "dealership row" was a natural place to begin selling used cars. Because there were many dealers close by, the Executive Leasing used car lot attracted many potential customers. But because the competitive environ-

ment was so intense, Jack thought carefully about a sales technique that would differentiate his company from the other sellers of used cars. His idea was to establish a fixed price — fair but firm — and stick to it. That fixed price would not only differentiate his business from his competitors, but it would also accomplish another important objective, having the customer leave with a sense of having received fair treatment.

In the beginning both Jack's own managers and the customers were skeptical. People were well-conditioned to the process of dickering over the price of a used car. Whether that process was pleasant or unpleasant, people expected to go through it. When they discovered that there was no bargaining for these cars, first they reacted with surprise or disbelief, then

with suspicion — things simply weren't done that way. With the fixed-price system, customers had to study the differences between cars very carefully in order to evaluate price differences — a skill not many customers had. It was new and different, and many customers were not convinced that it resulted in a better deal.

The managers and salesmen who worked for Ray Covington had a hard time with the fixed-price system when it was first implemented. They had to deal directly with confused or frustrated customers, and the competition from established used car dealers was very tough. Other dealerships used loss leaders in their advertising (one or two cars priced very low to get readers' attention) in an effort to undermine Executive's fixed-price system.

Covington was known at Enterprise as "Whitey" to those who had earned their stripes and knew how to sell cars. His hair had turned prematurely gray, and each day he came to work with it meticulously combed. He was a skillful coach, teaching "green" salesmen the techniques of selling used cars. His role as coach was critical, since the sales technique the company used — the fixed-price system — was fundamentally different from the prevailing industry practice. He helped new employees who were trying to learn how to deal with customers, and once a bond of trust existed, he was no longer "Ray" but both a mentor and friend called "Whitey."

Jack committed the company to the fixed-price system because he believed it would be a successful long-term strategy in differentiating his business from his competitors. He also felt that it was fair and would build customer loyalty. Buying used cars had become a contest of wills, and he felt intuitively that, given the opportunity, many people would be relieved to avoid that system. He knew it would not be universally popular, but his goal was to increase his base of satisfied customers. He was adamant from the start that "fixed price" meant exactly what it said.

In 1966 Jack asked Don Ross, who had excelled in every assignment he had been given, to sell used cars downtown, in addition to running the rapidly expanding downtown rental business. Ross agreed, and Jack explained the fixed-price system carefully to him. Ross soon had to

test the limits of the fixed-price policy. After one particularly difficult negotiation with a customer, the customer agreed to buy a car, but insisted that the price be $5 less than the posted fixed price, saying he simply did not ever pay list price. Ross went inside to talk to his manager, saying he was willing to take the $5 out of his own commission in order to make the deal work.

In the summer of 1965 this advertisement was an early start in promoting the 1966 car models. Building customer interest before the fall arrival of the new models became a regular marketing activity for Executive Leasing and for other car dealers. The ad at right stresses the extra service Executive provided customers, assuring an easy transition into a leased car.

The manager said to Ross, "We'd better call Jack." Jack's response was, "Do not discount the price of that car. Our policy is that the price is the price, and that's it." Ross held firm, the customer left and the fixed-price policy

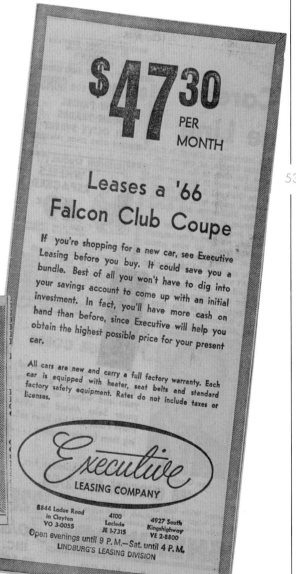

53

became even more firmly entrenched.

To Jack it was not simply a unique pricing policy, it was a continuing effort to treat the customer fairly and respectfully. Not only did the customers have to adjust to this new customer service approach, the salesmen

and managers had to adjust as well. One day Ross, who remained eager to sell used cars, put glow-in-the-dark streamers on the antennas of all of his used cars, imitating the tactics of other used car dealers. As soon as Jack saw the streamers, he said, "Get those things off. We don't want to look like other used car operations. We want to be different. People will know we're different because we will treat them right." Ross quickly took down all the streamers, and the business managed to grow

In 1964 one of the rental managers felt that renting campers offered an important new marketing potential for Executive Leasing. Jack agreed to give it a try, but soon discovered that the vehicles were more trouble than they were worth. Mechanical problems were a constant issue — the quality of the product was a far cry from what emerged in later years — and only a few units were leased. After about a year the camper effort was discontinued and Executive Leasing stuck to its knitting by doing what it knew best, leasing cars.

54

vigorously without them.

Jack's prediction was right. Eventually customers came to see the fixed-price approach as an advantage, and the Executive Leasing team came across as being on the customer's side, not a difficult adversary. Once the customers got over the initial surprise of a fixed price, their gratitude was made clear as the company's used car sales grew rapidly. Several decades later, other sellers of used cars moved to the fixed-price system, but not before Enterprise had become the largest seller of used cars to dealers, wholesalers and individuals in the U.S.

PREPARING FOR THE FUTURE

By the mid-1960s Executive Leasing had three locations and three lines of business. Leasing cars to individual customers remained the predominant business, but foundations had been put in place both for the daily rental business and for used car sales. The Clayton office continued to grow, and by the time they moved out of the "lower level" into new offices on Ladue Road, Jack and his team had taken over several more bays of the body shop and some space in an office building next door on Carondelet Avenue. They had built a fast-growing business.

Now there were well over 30 filing cabinets of documents and records, a very visible change from Ruby Garrison's one original filing cabinet. A computer service bureau was used to process much of the administrative work. All of the updates regarding the fleet and the leases had to be in by the 25th of each month so new printouts would be available for billing and for keeping all the individual car records current. It was a labor-intensive administrative system, one that often meant working on holidays and weekends. But it worked, and the administrative support kept up with the early growth of the leasing, rental and used car sales businesses.

Warren Knaup was hired by Jack in 1964 to manage the finance and accounting functions. Knaup began installing a system that provided management reports on a branch-by-branch basis, reports that calculated revenue and expense on a per-car basis. This information enabled Jack to measure the performance of different people and different offices in a consistent manner. Branch information was shared throughout the company, so each branch knew how it stacked up to the others.

These systems also fostered the internal sharing of performance information. Monthly meetings were held to share performance data and to highlight successes and shortcomings. Managers and salespeople liked the openness of the reports. They eagerly awaited each month's numbers, fostering a healthy competitive spirit. No one wanted to be on the bottom of the monthly performance reports.

This approach to measuring and reporting performance laid the groundwork for a performance-based compensation plan. It also kept people on their toes, because managers knew how their performance compared to the performance of their peers. It was like reading the baseball standings in the morning paper. They knew how they had done and how others had done, and these competitive managers were never comfortable being in the cellar.

These systems also enabled Jack and his management team to evaluate risk. With carefully prepared performance reports, they could then consider various "what if" questions. What if we changed the fleet size? What if we hired more people? What if we opened up out-of-town? That carefully constructed ability to analyze risk factors helped lay the groundwork for the growth that lay ahead.

The Buckhead office of Enterprise in Atlanta, which opened in 1969, was a first in more ways than one. It was the first office outside of St. Louis, it was the first office to carry the Enterprise name and it was the first office with an upscale style unlike the familiar scene of "dealership row." Opposite: Bruce Kruenegel's business card carried the Enterprise name into Kansas City. As the Atlanta and Kansas City offices began to grow, the formula for success that had been developed in St. Louis worked elsewhere, and the Enterprise green "e" became an increasingly familiar symbol in the car business.

$\mathcal{L}$AUNCHING ENTERPRISE BEYOND ST. LOUIS

ENTERPRISE LEASING COMPANY

7800 Metcalf Ave.
Overland Park, KS 66204   **BRUCE W. KRUENEGEL**
913-383-1300   Rental Manager

Throughout the 1960s the leasing business in St. Louis grew steadily, while the rental business inched along at a slower pace. Jack became immersed in leasing, and increasingly he traveled out of town to talk to other leasing people and to attend industry meetings. He gradually began to feel that the successful leasing business that was growing in St. Louis could be replicated elsewhere. His basic business principle was becoming entrenched in the minds of his managers: treat others as one would like to be treated. The early success of Executive Leasing grew out of strict adherence to his concept of customer service, and the concept was certainly portable.

As part of Jack's travel pattern during Andy and Jo Ann's school years, the family had taken regular vacation trips south, in large part because Jack hated cold weather. They drove from St. Louis to Florida, and Jack began to feel comfortable with the business climate and the weather in the Southeast.

By the early 1970s Jack Taylor was the majority owner of the company. He had expanded Executive's range of services to include used car sales and rentals. He would soon take the company into new geographic markets, as well.

ATLANTA: GATEWAY TO GROWTH

By 1969 Jack was eager to open a new location outside of St. Louis. He had spent a great deal of time thinking about site characteristics he felt would be important for success, and he felt the company was strong enough to handle a new venture. In deciding where to go, Jack had two priorities: to pick a city somewhat like St. Louis and to pick a manager with strong leasing experience who wanted to run it. He narrowed the list of cities down to Kansas City and Atlanta and then chose a manager who was eager to move. After deciding that Don Nations would start the new office, he asked Don to visit Kansas City and Atlanta. Jack wanted Nations to have a role in making the final decision about the location — starting up in a new city would be tough, and Jack wanted the manager to buy into the decision.

Nations told Jack he felt that Atlanta was the place to go, and Jack agreed. The rationale for Atlanta was more intuitive than rational. In many respects, Atlanta was like St. Louis. At the time it was a relaxed town, a second-tier city without the frantic, competitive pace of New York, Chicago or Los Angeles. It was grow-

ing at a steady rate with what appeared to be a stable economy, and the people were friendly. Nice people with steady jobs seemed to be good prospects for a leasing business with a heavy emphasis on customer service. The warm weather was an added benefit, and Southern hospitality was certainly consistent with Jack's way of doing business.

For over 10 years Jack had built his management team by carefully recruiting inexperienced people who were willing to learn to do business his way and then delegating substantial responsibilities to them. He trained them carefully, and as they matured in the business, his confidence in them grew. During the early years Jack watched the company's growth accelerate as he delegated large parts of the business to seasoned managers. He had discovered that delegating to people whom he trusted was the best way to break out of the small company mold that could constrain the growth he was eager to foster. He broke through the barrier that holds back many entrepreneurs: unwillingness to give up complete control. Early on he learned to share responsibility with carefully chosen colleagues who had developed into "young Jack Taylors" in the way they thought about the business.

The expansion into Atlanta was not part of a long-range plan for the business, but was a pragmatic decision based on what Jack thought was likely to work. The risk was considered carefully, and Jack knew that if the move didn't work out, it would not wreck the company. Going to Atlanta was a measured leap of faith. When this sturdy little St. Louis-based company took that huge leap into the heartland of Dixie, there was no sense of how vast the frontier was for future growth. For Jack the move was a way to build the business and provide more opportunities for his managers, as well as a reason to travel south. He had no premonition that this was the first step toward becoming an international company.

A NEW NAME

One of the first issues to arise in conjunction with the opening of the Atlanta office was the company's name. Executive Leasing was already being used by an established Atlanta company. Jack had to use another name in Atlanta, and he wanted a name that had some connection with himself and with Executive Leasing.

His first thought was to preserve the "e" logo. He liked the look of the logo and had grown very comfortable with it in St. Louis. He liked it on signs, stationery and business cards, and it had become the signature for the company. If he couldn't use the same name out of town, at least he could use the same logo.

The "e" logo also had strong personal associations. The brother of Don Holtzmann, the man who had started the car rental business for Jack, had asked Jack years earlier if he could use the Executive name as part of a college graphics project. Jack was pleased that Holtzmann's brother had shown interest in his company, and he asked him to show him his work when it was completed. The finished design looked good to Jack. He asked the man if he could buy it and use it for the company, and the man agreed.

Once he knew that he wanted to use the logo, he then had to come up with a name starting with "e." His first thought was "Essex" since that was the name of the aircraft carrier on which he had spent most of his combat time during the war. The Essex name, however, sounded too heavy, like something large and ponderous, and that was not what his company stood for.

The other name from Jack's navy days was "Enterprise," the other carrier on which he had served a short period of time. Enterprise felt right, both because of the sentimental attachment and because of what it stood for — an effort that requires boldness and energy. That was what his company was all about. The Atlanta office was named Enterprise Leasing, and the St. Louis offices continued to be Executive Leasing. (All of the subsequent

By the 1970s the "e" logo had emerged as the unifying identification mark for all the Enterprise offices, both leasing and rental. The two-color style used earlier to differentiate leasing from rental had given way to one color — Enterprise green. The easy-flowing style of the logo was a subtle understatement of the fast pace at which the Enterprise team was moving.

59

ENTERPRISE
EPIGRAMS

YOUR BEST CUSTOMER IS
YOUR COMPETITION'S BEST PROSPECT.

In the days before advanced technology made keeping track of cars simpler, Enterprise employees like Bob Klaskin and Karen Lea, below, kept the manual systems up to date. The chalkboard tracked the date cars went out on rental and when they were due back, as well as the scheduled maintenance for the entire fleet. The familiar "key board" on the side wall kept the car keys quickly available. The rental employee at right checking under the hood of the car was doing in the late 1960s what rental employees still do worldwide — monitoring maintenance and using the ever-present vacuum that sucks up trash and ties. The Enterprise epigram above sums up the motivation of these hard-working employees.

60

out-of-town locations of the company were named Enterprise Leasing. In 1978 the St. Louis offices were renamed and they became Enterprise Leasing offices. In 1989 the company name was changed to Enterprise Rent-A-Car Company.)

SLOW GROWTH IN THE SOUTH

Even with a professional image, a new name and an eagerness to write car leases, Enterprise found the progress slow in Atlanta. Leasing was still a new phenomenon, and an out-of-town company had to work hard for the word-of-mouth publicity that had come quickly in St. Louis. Progress over the first two years was uneven.

Jack was concerned about the pace of growth, but he continued to feel that the business could be made to work in Atlanta. Warren Knaup, Jack's chief financial officer, made regular trips to Atlanta to monitor the financial condition of that office. Knaup methodically evaluated all aspects of the operation to learn what was working and what was wrong.

It became apparent that while part of the problem was a marketing effort without clear focus, another part of

the problem was the very nature of the leasing business. By its nature, the leasing business takes a long time to become profitable — income is realized gradually during the several years of the lease, and much of the income occurs when the car is sold at the end of the lease. With a small fleet of cars on lease, profits inevitably come slowly.

After a few years of inconsistent progress, a new manager was sent to run the Atlanta office. Bill Lortz was a veteran manager in St. Louis who had a strong marketing track record as a branch manager, and he was also known for his tenacious attention to details. Jack had first approached Bill about running the Atlanta office in 1969, but — as remained company policy — the decision was left to Bill.

The Courtland Street office in downtown Atlanta continued the steady expansion of the business out of town. This was the second location in Atlanta, and it is still a busy office today. Atlanta was the first place the Enterprise name was used because another company had already claimed the name Executive Leasing.

61

He had declined Jack's offer in 1969 because he and his wife, Lainey, just had a new baby, but in 1973 Jack knew the Atlanta office needed him badly. When Jack asked him at Christmas time in 1973 if he would run the Atlanta office, he quickly accepted the job and started work in Atlanta right after the holidays.

Both Jack and Lortz felt that the Atlanta office could become successful. For the first few months, Lortz concentrated on learning what was needed in order to make the leasing business in Atlanta work. Jack's view was that the basic principles of the business worked well in St. Louis and they should work well in Atlanta. Lortz had to find out if that was right. He knew that successful marketing was the critical factor in generating a large portfolio of well-structured leases to creditworthy customers.

Lortz was initially told that people in Atlanta didn't wear a coat and tie to work on Saturday mornings. He was skeptical, feeling that the dress code had always made a huge difference in the image Enterprise put in front of its customers. One Saturday morning he took his salespeople to Rich's department store in Atlanta. When he showed his people that the Rich's sales-

people wore coats and ties, the message took hold. There was no further debate about the image of Enterprise in Atlanta. He managed by example — showing his people how to make it work — and the Atlanta office began to turn steadily profitable. Lortz demonstrated that the success was in the details — focus on creditworthy customers, present yourself professionally and only bite off as much business as you can chew.

It was also in Atlanta that the potential of the rental business became apparent. Contrary to the experience in St. Louis, the rental business grew much faster than the leasing business. People in Atlanta were used to buying cars rather than leasing them, and Lortz had found that while the leasing business grew slowly without strong word-of-mouth support, rentals, on the other hand, moved very quickly. With Atlanta's strong economy and its many families with two working spouses, the likely need for a replacement rental car stimulated the Enterprise rental business.

The rental business was focused on the local in-town market rather than the airport, and the rental fleet grew quickly. Jack had made the decision earlier that he would avoid the airport

rental business in St. Louis, and as the rental business expanded out of town, he decided that this strategy was an important one to keep. The airport business had a fierce competitiveness that was based much more on price than on customer service. The Enterprise philosophy about business, however, was to build a strong base of customers who would keep coming back because they liked the way they were treated. Jack knew it would have been difficult for Enterprise to distinguish itself from competitors at airports, where car rentals were more like a commodity.

Atlanta demonstrated that there was less competition for the suburban rental business and that customer service was a critical factor in getting and keeping that business. With a strong branch manager pushing aggressively, it was soon clear that the potential for rentals, especially in fast-growing cities, was vast. Lortz was a forceful leader, and the renewed effort in Atlanta soon paid off. He focused on high-quality credit standards for leasing and rental customers and set regular, achievable goals for growth. The base of business that was now growing in Atlanta included both leasing and rental customers, and the base was solid. The foundation Lortz built served both to turn the office around to profitability and to prepare it to weather the as-yet-unforeseen energy crisis looming around the corner.

"When Bill set his jaw, he looked like a face on Mount Rushmore," said one of his managers. "But he was always there for all of us and would give us the shirt off his back."

ORLANDO: THE START OF SOMETHING BIG

Even though the results in Atlanta were inconsistent during the first two years, by 1971 Jack was ready to open another office. Years earlier, when Arthur Lindburg had urged Jack to expand into downtown St. Louis before the Clayton office reached a comfortable level of sustained profitability, Jack had reluctantly agreed. His doubts had been put to rest by the success of the downtown office. That experience gave him confidence to expand before reaching a level of complete comfort, but it meant that he considered the risk carefully. Some level of risk was always involved in the establishment of a new office; after all, a new office has to have time to build its own track record. Jack's policy was to take on a certain

amount of risk, but without betting the company's future.

By 1971 there were five offices in St. Louis and one in Atlanta, and the largest rental fleet was 85 cars at one office in St. Louis. The Southeast felt comfortable to Jack, and he decided the next state he wanted to open in was Florida. Building on what was working in St. Louis and Atlanta, Jack looked for a mid-sized city where he felt comfortable competitively. Enterprise's accounting firm told Jack that Orlando was expected to grow dramatically since the opening of the Walt Disney World Resort would bring new jobs. Jack was convinced that Orlando was the best place for Enterprise to put its toe in the water in Florida.

Jack always felt that if people could choose what they wanted to do, there was a much greater likelihood that they would succeed. For that reason, during this expansion period Jack asked people if they would like to move elsewhere, rather than simply telling them they were being transferred. Jack had watched Bob Bell's performance as a leasing manager in St. Louis and felt very comfortable with Bell's approach to the business. He

Expansion required a few unifying traditions be instituted. The Enterprise "e" proved an important symbol of the company and found its way onto numerable objects around Enterprise offices, including employees via these ties and cravats.

Don and Nancy Ross settled into Kansas City expecting it to be their home for many years to come. Periodic managers' seminars took them to St. Louis and to a few sunny spots to convene with other Enterprise managers and spouses, like Van and Marion Black, right. As the business in Kansas grew, Don looked toward other cities. On one trip to Topeka, he and Nancy left their three boys at home and did some sightseeing, below, as they looked for potential new Enterprise locations.

asked Bell if he would be interested in opening an office in Orlando. Bell quickly agreed.

Jack then asked Lanny Dacus if he would like to go to Florida with Bell to manage the rental business in Orlando. Dacus, unlike Bell, was a newcomer to the company, having been on the job in St. Louis for less than a year, but his manner with people seemed to be the right fit for the rental business even though his tenure was short. Dacus agreed to the move, and the Florida expansion got underway. Neither Jack nor his managers had any clue when

they opened in Florida that their entry into that market would transform Enterprise into a rental company and would be the springboard for explosive growth.

STRONG ROOTS GROW
A HEALTHY BUSINESS

With the expansion in the Southeast under way, in 1972 Jack turned again to Kansas City. He asked Don Ross whether he'd be interested in going to Kansas City to open a leasing office. Ross had already accumulated significant experience in St. Louis in leasing, rental and used car sales. Ross agreed, and once in Kansas City, he initially worked from an upstairs bedroom until he found a location for an office. The

first Kansas City office was an old Texaco gas station that had been gutted. Ross and his salesmen wrote leases and rented cars from a folding card table in that gas station before essential renovations could be completed.

Though Kansas City was very similar to St. Louis, when Ross settled into the new office, the phone did not ring. People had never heard of Enterprise, and Ross quickly realized that this new venture would have to create its own reputation. Developing a local business meant becoming part of the local community. He started hiring people from Kansas City (some of the first local hires in Kansas City are still with Enterprise in Kansas City today), and he got involved in the business community.

First he opened a local bank

account and told the bank that Enterprise was there to be a local company, not just to generate profits for St. Louis. Then he quickly developed relationships with the local car dealers, many of whom were eager to involve Ross in local activities. In short order he was on the board of the Chamber of Commerce, he became president of the Overland Park Business Association and he ran the Fall Festival Parade. As the local roots grew deeper, the Enterprise business in Kansas City grew stronger.

In the first months in Kansas City, Ross had a regular Tuesday morning phone conversation with Jack and Warren Knaup to go over the progress of the week. They reviewed deals that had been finalized and plans in the works for new business. Ross had managed an office in St. Louis and was comfortable talking both about the big picture issues and about the details of daily operations.

In one of their Tuesday conversations, Knaup asked Ross about the gross profit return on a new lease that had been written on a Suburban vehicle that Ross had leased to the head of a local business. Suburbans were not on the standard rate lists, so Ross had calculated the rate manually, a task that he had done frequently in the past. As he explained to Knaup the way he had constructed the lease, it quickly became apparent he had made a mathematical error.

"When I carried everything forward on the sheets," Ross explained to Jack, "for some reason, I didn't pick up the interest cost on a monthly basis. Now I see it. I have no gross in this; it's a break-even deal. What do you want me to do?"

"Nothing," said Jack. "You made a mistake. It's okay. I appreciate that you told me the straight story. Mistakes happen, learn from it and move on." Jack's confidence in his managers was one of the reasons the expansion process went so smoothly.

Don Ross was big on flags. "I always flew the American flag at home," says Ross, "and I thought we should fly flags at the office." Overland Park was the first office in Kansas City, and when it was remodeled as the group headquarters some years later, a flag pole was installed so that American and Enterprise flags would fly side-by-side every day. When Ross left Kansas City to return to St. Louis, he was given the Enterprise flag, an appropriate memento for the man who carried the Enterprise flag into new territory. Part of forging into new territory was scouting missions to new cities. On these trips Don Ross lived out of his trunk, as did other managers as the years progressed.

These two shots of the Overland Park office show the dramatic growth of the Kansas City location in the few years from its opening in the early 1970s to the mid-1970s. During Enterprise's early expansion, many new offices were modest, sometimes ramshackle buildings, that made the same transformation as Enterprise took hold in the new location. Enterprise's leasing business still had top billing, but the rental business was definitely influencing the speed at which Enterprise was growing.

*B*ruce Kruenegel moved to Kansas City from St. Louis when Don Ross opened the first Kansas City office. Kruenegel was the business manager in Kansas City, a tough job at a time when there were few guidelines about running the business out-of-town. He stayed in close touch with managers in St. Louis, particularly Warren Knaup in the early days. Kruenegel remained in Kansas City until he transferred several years later to Chicago as the city rental manager. The "small city" backdrop shown in this photo of the office in downtown Kansas City was a preview of later expansion efforts in top-tier cities.

As the expansion continued outside of St. Louis with the Enterprise name gradually taking hold elsewhere, the Executive name stayed in use in St. Louis. These ads for holiday rental specials in 1975 kept the rental business linked with the leasing business for name recognition purposes. Just as Executive Leasing had originally been linked with the well-established Lindburg Cadillac business, the new rental business was linked with what was by the mid-1970s the well-established Executive Leasing business in St. Louis.

The early 1970s were difficult years for Ross to start a new office in Kansas City. The energy crisis brought with it long lines at gas stations, and double-digit interest rates caused consumer confidence to plummet. Jack visited Kansas City whenever Ross wanted to talk, and he reinforced the strategy of sticking to the basics. He also pointed out tactical steps that could alleviate certain pressures created by the fast-changing world of high rates and limited gasoline: while some of the larger cars Ross was holding to resell had declined in value, other smaller cars were worth nearly their entire original sales price at resale.

Often in his visits to Kansas City, Jack asked Ross, "What do you think you're going to do next month?" They talked back and forth, Ross thinking on his feet, Jack trying to anticipate the trends in the business. Often those conversations turned into forecasts for the business, but they were always small bites. The plan was to stretch for business, but only to reach for what was reasonable.

Ross was determined to hit any target he set. Since times were tough with rationed gas and high interest rates, it meant that it took even more work to lease and rent cars. Milestones were small, and there were no home runs.

After one particularly tough day, Ross got home late feeling exhausted and elated. "I leased three more cars today, and all of our rental cars are out. I had a great day," Ross exclaimed to his wife, Nancy, when he got home. "Yay!" was the quick shout from his three sons, and there then followed a parade through the house with the kids banging pots and pans and shouting, "Dad had a great day, Yay!..."

Ross had more and more great days as the leasing and rental businesses both grew slowly but steadily. His early experience in Kansas City demonstrated that the autonomy of running the local business could work well when coupled with clear measures

of performance and heavy doses of managerial and moral support when needed.

The team that Ross built in Kansas City combined people from St. Louis and people from Kansas City. By the late 1970s the team was well established, and many members of that Kansas City team later moved on to jobs elsewhere. Susie Irwin, who was hired in Kansas City in 1979, was among the first women hired by Enterprise to work in a rental position. She started as a management trainee, and like all trainees — male or female — her work ranged from filling out rental contracts to vacuuming cars. Her skills grew rapidly, and she moved first to Houston and then became a vice president and general manager in Sacramento, California. As a married mother of two children, she was an early role model for many other women who have moved through the ranks at Enterprise.

By the time Ross left Kansas City to return to St. Louis in 1980, the Enterprise presence was well entrenched there with five offices, over 1,000 cars on lease, and a rental fleet of 500 cars. That business had been built one customer and one car at a time, and its foundation was solid.

The SUPPORTIVE *Spouse*

As the company began to experience fast-paced growth, the role of the manager's spouse became critical for success. Just as in the early days when Mary Ann Taylor accompanied Jack on repossession missions, numerous other women played crucial roles in the early history, doing work that had to be done if the business were to succeed. The work was hard, and the hours were long for the managers, all of whom were men in the early days. The support of the wife was essential, both at home and at work.

Mary Ann Taylor continued to be the "First Lady" of the company throughout this period. She was always there for picnics and Christmas parties and was always ready to talk with the wife whose husband had just been transferred into a new and confusing role.

But Mary Ann's role was more than that of pouring coffee and providing a sympathetic ear. She understood the business, and she knew firsthand the impact of its growth. She was able to explain to other wives what was going on, why Jack felt so strongly about customer service, why it was crucial to build business fast in a new location before the competition woke up and why you had to repossess cars as soon as payments were delinquent.

Over the years she no longer was able to know every wife by name (just as Jack no longer knew every employee by name). At one Christmas party, when the crowd had grown large with new faces, she overheard one woman say to another, "There is Mrs. Cheese." Baffled by being referred to as Mrs. Cheese, she asked a friend what that meant. "Oh, some of the guys call Jack 'the Big Cheese,' so I guess that makes you Mrs. Cheese." Mary Ann knew that the small leasing business from Clayton would never be the same.

The first Enterprise location in Florida opened when the flag was planted at 35 East Colonial Drive in Orlando. The large green "e" was erected at the front of the car lot with a wide array of cars easily visible. The business in Florida was both leasing and rental when it first opened, but it was the rental business that exploded and put Enterprise on the map. Opposite: Lanny Dacus was the tenacious manager of the rental business when it opened in Florida, and as he pounded the streets for business, he learned that unsurpassed customer service was what made Enterprise succeed.

Chapter Five

THE RENTAL BUSINESS TAKES OFF

Each Enterprise location and each manager developed a different strategy for growth. The combination of individual personalities and local and regional markets created a unique opportunity for each of these early expansion efforts. Sending Lanny Dacus to Orlando as the rental manager, for instance, was an exception to Jack's established practice of relying on experienced managers who had worked with him for years.

Dacus had been hired by Executive Leasing when he was 30, having previously run his own ice cream parlor, which was across the street from the South Kingshighway office. He had been with Executive less than a year when he was offered the Orlando position. His gritty determination and creative thinking had quickly earned Jack's confidence. When he was first interviewed by Executive Leasing, Dacus had wanted the job so passionately that he offered to work for six months with no pay in order to prove himself. Dacus was started at the going rate for new employees, but his tenacity made a big impact. His attitude, combined with beneficial legislation and a focused marketing effort, would make the expansion into Florida highly successful for the small but fast-growing leasing company from St. Louis.

A LANDSLIDE OF OPPORTUNITY

A few days after arriving in Orlando, Dacus called on a local insurance adjuster and described what Enterprise could do for him and his customers. The adjuster liked Dacus, perhaps because Dacus was persistent in a friendly way and because his Midwestern twang set him apart from others in Orlando. Dacus explained that the insurance replacement business was a high priority for Enterprise and detailed how it could benefit the adjuster's business.

Enterprise offered several programs that differentiated it from its competitors: unlimited mileage for insurance customers, direct billing to the insurance companies and waiving the 48-hour waiting period for thefts. (The first 48 hours after a theft were not covered by insurance companies since many stolen cars were recovered quickly, so Enterprise provided the first two days free.) Dacus's intense enthusiasm persuaded the adjuster that Enterprise, an unknown new company in town, deserved his business.

Then the adjuster did something totally unexpected that would put Dacus on the map in Florida — he offered to introduce him to other adjusters. It was as though Lanny Dacus, this friendly but unknown man from far away, had passed the initiation ritual and was being taken into a close-knit club, a club in which personal relationships and introductions make it easier to do business. The word-of-mouth advertising that had been so critical in the early days in St. Louis was now working for Dacus in Orlando — every adjuster he called had already heard about him and greeted him, "Hi, Lanny, come on in." The rental business got a jump-start from that adjuster and began to build quickly.

The primary competitors for local rental business in Orlando at that time were the new car dealers. Some of those dealerships had 100 to 200 rental cars, and they competed aggressively for the insurance replacement business. Their rates were low, subsidized by the manufacturer, but their service was limited. The other car rental companies, many of whom had more financial muscle than Enterprise, had chosen different strategies and concentrated on airport and tourist business rather than insurance replacement business. The timing was perfect for Enterprise to move aggressively in the insurance replacement niche.

The Orlando office opened in mid-September 1971, and Jack asked Lanny Dacus how many cars he would have in the rental fleet by December. Dacus told Jack he would have 50 cars by December. At the time the largest rental fleet in any Enterprise office was 85 cars. Dacus went out on a limb when he said he would hit 50 cars within 90 days, but he was convinced that the connections made through the insurance adjuster would enable him to build the fleet at a near-record rate.

Jack often nudged his managers by asking how much business they thought they could do in the near future. Very often, as with Dacus, the managers stretched their own personal goals whenever the boss questioned what they could do. Jack's instinct was that a manager would work harder to achieve a personal goal, even a stretched goal, than to achieve a goal mandated by someone else. It was then a goal that was owned by the manager, and all the stops would be pulled to achieve it.

Lanny had been optimistic with his estimate of future business, but he was helped to his goal by the Florida legislature. In January 1972 a no-fault insurance law went into effect in Florida that mandated that insurance companies had to provide replacement cars to anyone in an accident, regardless of fault. Suddenly the insurance companies and the body shops were overwhelmed with business, and the car rental business exploded. Though the law was repealed within a year, it changed the habits of consumers when it came time for car repairs. The Orlando Enterprise office increased its fleet to 185 cars within four months, an unprecedented event in the company.

THE RENTAL BUSINESS TAKES PRIORITY

Once Dacus knew that the favorable insurance law was soon to be repealed, he encouraged Jack to expand in Florida while the consumer pattern for rentals was still strong. In 1972 the insurance companies were pushing Dacus to go to Tampa since they all had large operations there and were very pleased with the relationship with Enterprise in Orlando. Having worked with the adjusters for over a year, he not only had gained their personal friendships, but now he had earned his professional stripes by delivering the cars and the service they wanted.

Jack had watched the rental business skyrocket in Orlando, and from his own frequent visits to Florida, he

SPECIAL
Delivery®

Because Orlando was growing so quickly and because the consumers' need for rental cars skyrocketed after the change in the insurance law, the Enterprise office had more customers than it could handle. Lanny Dacus had printed cards for the insurance adjusters with maps to guide their customers to Enterprise, and customers came in droves. With the change in the law, consumers quickly realized car repairs could be easier on them if they used a rental car paid for by their insurance company. The arrival of Enterprise in Florida was perfectly timed to take advantage of this surge in demand for rental cars.

Soon Dacus started going out to pick up customers. He knew that he could even out the flow of customers and prevent crowded counters in the office by scheduling pickups at times convenient for him. The times convenient for him were often first thing in the morning or late in the day, which were also convenient times for people with busy work schedules. Little did they realize that these "special deliveries" were not so much for their benefit as to help Dacus when he was short-handed.

When Jack learned about the customer pickups, he called Dacus. "You need to watch that. I don't want you to offer anything we can't provide when we get bigger. Whatever you start today, we have to continue." Jack made clear to Dacus that they had to understand the downside risk as well as the upside potential. Dacus continued the program, increasingly confident that it would boost his success.

The story spread throughout the company. The first reaction was incredulous —

"Has Lanny lost his mind?" Then, as more and more managers thought about the rationale behind the pickup program, it began to spread to Enterprise offices in other cities. What started as a spur-of-the-moment solution to a logistical problem became a mainstay of the marketing program for the Enterprise rental business. The Special Delivery program would be depicted as the car wrapped in brown packing paper as the focus of a national advertising campaign many years later.

74

The first location in Tampa was 3909 Hillsborough Avenue. When this office opened, it was the first Enterprise location anywhere to open for the sole purpose of doing rental business and was a small first omen of the future evolution of Enterprise as a car rental company. This Tampa office is still active today after several remodelings.

felt that there was much potential for quick growth in the rental business in other parts of the state. Dacus, too, had seen the rental business explode in Orlando, and he began investigating Tampa on his own. Every Saturday Dacus ran the Orlando rental office until 1:00 p.m., and then he drove to Tampa. Week after week he kept up the routine, usually getting home well after midnight. His on-the-scene evaluation of the Tampa market confirmed that the company should open an office in Tampa as quickly as possible.

After learning the local geography, Dacus found a three-bay Standard Oil service station that was for sale. The price was $89,000, Jack agreed to buy it, and Enterprise was committed to Tampa. Dacus sketched the renovation plan with his kids' crayons and sent it to Jack for approval. Jack's reply was, "Okay, do it."

Dacus promoted Dick Rush to rental manager in Orlando as his replacement when he moved his family to Tampa. Dick Rush had been born and raised in Orlando and knew his way around that city very well. Once the Tampa office was under way, it

grew even faster than Orlando — Tampa grew its rental fleet a car a day for the first 180 days, and it was profitable its second month. Dacus and his wife, Melanie, who played a large part in his success, delivered cars to customers until after 8:00 at night several nights a week with their kids in tow in the back seat. The Enterprise reputation had taken hold in Florida, and no competitor could match their tenacious determination to rent cars.

The Tampa office was the first office in the history of Enterprise to open as a non-leasing branch. Its sole business was rental, and its quick success astounded — and frustrated — many of the longer-term leasing managers in the company. Leasing had

This rate card combined the now-familiar green "e" logo with the Enterprise Rent-A-Car name. It also promoted use of an "800" number, another small step toward what would eventually become a major way of doing business as the rental business exploded nationwide.

When Enterprise opened its 100th office in Pompano Beach, Florida, the milestone was celebrated throughout the company. This simple commemorative gift, given to all employees nationwide in May 1983, marked the success of the moment but left room for bigger celebrations of the company's astonishing growth in the following decades.

always been the company's core business, but its very nature meant that it took a significant investment of money and time for a new office to become profitable. Some people in the company were beginning to feel threatened by the large, quick profits that the upstart rental business was generating. Others were more subtle in their disdain for the rental business, simply waiting for it to fail so Enterprise would resume its historical emphasis on leasing.

It did not fail. Instead the daily rental business continued to grow, and once again Dacus started investigating a new market. For six months, Dacus drove from Tampa to Jacksonville on Saturday afternoons, driving around to learn a new city and getting home after midnight. He found three potential locations in Jacksonville, and Jack and Earl Lindburg flew in to look at all of them. They agreed with the one Dacus favored.

Dacus moved once again, though there was still no company policy on relocating — he paid for the move and

settled in to repeat his earlier successes in Jacksonville. Jacksonville progressed even faster than Tampa, growing more than a car a day in the first 180 days. Though the insurance law had been repealed, consumers had gotten used to the replacement cars, and many insurance companies continued to offer them as additional coverage on individual policies. Enterprise's rental business continued to grow.

Throughout the Florida expansion, Jack supported and encouraged Dacus and the other Enterprise people in Florida, and as a result, he moved them to a higher level of performance. These employees came to expect more of themselves, and as they continued to establish their own goals, those goals moved higher and higher. They strove to be like Jack, with the same sense of dedication, loyalty and work ethic, and Jack treated them as friends as well as employees. They grew in their jobs with creative hard work, and they all shared in the benefits.

Success Hits a Speed Bump

Dacus pushed for further expansion in Florida, advocating either Miami or Fort Lauderdale. None of the Enterprise senior managers wanted to go to

*S*unrise Boulevard was the first office in South Florida. Just as Enterprise had done in Atlanta, as the company grew throughout Florida it tried to keep a close rein on the costs of expansion and yet still fit with the local style. This office had been a Krystal Hamburger restaurant in its earlier life before Enterprise claimed it as another office, much to the surprise of some of the neighbors.

Miami — it was different from all the other places where they did business, a faster pace and full of tougher competition. Jack was still not ready to take on a big city. Relying on his usual method of weekend exploration, Dacus finally located a site in Fort Lauderdale: an empty Krystal Hamburger restaurant, available for rent at $1,000 per month.

Jack agreed to the site but was not willing to commit to a five-year lease. After lengthy negotiations, the parties agreed on a clause that came to be known within Enterprise as the "JCT clause." That clause provided that by giving 90 days notice and paying 90 days of additional rent, the lease could be terminated by Enterprise. Variations of the "JCT clause" became the standard procedure within the company for limiting downside risk on new, unproved expansion locations.

Dacus moved to Fort Lauderdale in 1975, and for the first time, the business did not go well. In 30 days he had only rented three cars. Something fundamentally different was happening, and Dacus did not understand it.

What he did not understand was that South Florida was a very different market from Jacksonville. He had rolled into town, a cocky guy from Jacksonville in a three-piece suit, and

nothing had gone right. The second month he was there, he confided to an insurance adjuster that business was not going well and asked for some advice.

The adjuster's analysis was simple: "You're dressed wrong. None of us knew who you were when you first came in here. We thought you might be an Internal Revenue Service agent or something like that."

Dacus immediately realized that the way of doing business and the network of contacts he relied on in northern Florida simply did not work in South Florida. He went home, changed into a brown blazer and tan pants, and resumed his calls on the adjusters. This time the business took off, either because of the change in wardrobe or because Dacus had taken his approach down a notch and added a healthy dose of humility. It was simply a different town with a different attitude that slowed his initial success, not any fundamentals of the business itself.

Every time he had a tough sales call to make, Lanny put on his reliable brown blazer and tan pants, and the business began to grow. With his change in attitude, the business in Fort Lauderdale quickly fell into the same

rapid car-a-day growth patterns he had experienced in northern Florida. The combination of a temporary change in the law, rapid growth in population and a change in consumer patterns all came together throughout Florida during the 1970s for the Enterprise rental business. The company learned that its formula, which had been developed in St. Louis and now refined elsewhere, was solid. Its managers learned that they could beat their competitors by delivering creative, unsurpassed customer service. And they learned that not every market has identical attitudes and styles of doing business. By the mid-1970s Enterprise's rental business was rapidly gaining ground on the leasing business.

By the early 1980s Enterprise had a firm foothold in most of the major population centers in Florida. This infrastructure of offices became a solid foundation for the important growth of the rental business that took place throughout the 1980s. The growth of the rental business in Florida, and many of the marketing efforts that worked there, became a model for the emerging rental business in other parts of the country.

78

JACKSONVILLE

EAST
4303 Atlantic Blvd.
Jacksonville, Florida 32207
904-396-0339

WEST
1705 Cassat Avenue
Jacksonville, Florida 32210
904-388-3553

**ORLANDO
DOWNTOWN**
35 E. Colonial Drive
Orlando, Florida 32801
305-843-5411

NORTH
283 E. Highway 434
Suite 1
Longwood, Florida 32750
305-339-1199

WEST BALM BEACH
970 North Congress Ave
West Palm Beach, Florida 33409
305-689-8585

DEL-RAY BEACH
1980 S. Federal
Del-Ray Beach, Florida 33444
305-278-5200

FT. LAUDERDALE
1311 East Sunrise Blvd.
Ft. Lauderdale, Florida 33304
305-764-3144

HOLLYWOOD
1627 South 21st Ave.
Hollywood, Florida 33020
305-920-0444

**MIAMI
CENTRAL**
169 N.E. 29th Street
Miami, Florida 33137
305-576-1300

SOUTH
9300 South Dixie Highway
Miami, Florida 33156
305-667-1601

TARPON SPRINGS
(New Port Richey to Dunedin)
3760 U. S. Highway 19 North
Holiday, Florida 33589
813-934-6994

TAMPA WEST
3909 West Hillsborough Ave.
Tampa, Florida 33614
813-885-5636

TAMPA EAST
10552 North Florida Ave.
Tampa, Florida 33612
813-932-6170

ST. PETERSBURG - LARGO
8501 49th Street North
Pinellas Park, Florida 33565
813-544-2551

LAKELAND - WINTER HAVEN
2500 U.S. Highway 92 East
Lakeland, Florida 33801
813-665-2484

CLEARWATER - DUNEDIN
1943 U.S. Highway 19 North
Clearwater, Florida 33515
813-796-3442

BRADENTON - SARASOTA
5627 D. 14th Street West
Bradenton, Florida 33507
813-756-0602

FT. MYERS
(Port Charlotte to Naples)
4452 Cleveland Avenue
Ft. Myers, Florida 33901
813-936-8222

ENTERPRISE RENT-A-CAR
Division of Enterprise Leasing

There were literal and figurative dark clouds on the horizon as Enterprise's first expansion locations were taking hold. The energy crisis of the early 1970s wreaked havoc on various players in the automobile industry. But just as the devastation of real life tornadoes would bring the Enterprise team closer together, this nationwide energy crisis would forge a stronger Enterprise with a more diverse fleet and a renewed appreciation for its strong roots. Opposite: In contrast to Enterprise's staying power, an entire block of utility poles was torn down when this tornado hit St. Louis County in 1972.

$\mathscr{W}$EATHERING TURBULENT CHANGE

July 23, 1973, had been a normal day at the Clayton office on Ladue Road. The people in the leasing department had pretty much wrapped up the day. Van Black, one of the leasing salesmen, called his wife, Marion, to tell her he would be home shortly. Just as Marion told him to be careful, the sky darkened, and torrential rain began to pound on the roof of the building. Before they could hang up, the phone went dead.

At the same moment, leasing administrative assistant Brenda Haar left the office and hurried through the rain to her car. As she climbed in, she saw a huge funnel cloud across the street roaring toward the Enterprise building, tree limbs and debris flying through the air. She ran back inside and screamed, "A tornado is coming, a tornado is coming!!!"

81

In the early 1970s the Ladue Road offices of Executive Leasing had become the heart of the company's operations. Critical records were maintained there, and much of the corporate staff was located there. The 1973 storm left Executive Leasing crippled, but only briefly. Employees rallied, and the skills they developed would come in handy later as other storms rolled through what some called "tornado alley."

Buildings damaged, 35,000 homes powerless in storm

JUL 25 1973

Heavy rains and high winds caused extensive property damage and left 35,000 homes without power for several hours.

A spokesman for the Union Electric Co. reported that approximately 35,000 customers were without power as high winds caused damage to power lines beginning about 6 p.m. Monday. Hardest hit were the northern and northwestern portions of St. Louis County, according to the spokesman.

MOST OF THE homes had power restored within several hours but about 500 of them were without power for more than 12 hours, he said.

A warehouse and store of Jackman's Fabrics, 1234 North Lindbergh bl., suffered extensive damage when winds caused part of the roof to collapse. William Wolff, an employe, was pinned in the wreckage for 30 minutes before he was freed unharmed by firemen of the Creve Coeur Fire Protection District.

Bolts of fabrics stored in the warehouse were extensively damaged as rain poured in, according to a company spokesman.

OFFICES of the Executive Leasing Co., a car leasing firm at 8844 Ladue rd., Creve Coeur, also were damaged Monday, according to a company representative.

Part of the roof and the front portion of the building containing sales offices were damaged by rain and debris, the spokesman said.

Also damaged was the Barford Chevrolet Co., 8500 Maryland ave., Clayton.

The general manager of the company said seven large plateglass windows of the showroom were broken.

He also said 15 cars, some in the showroom, had broken windows and windshields caused by the storm.

LIGHTNING struck and toppled a 20-foot radio antenna atop the home of Curt McFerron of 11212 Natural Bridge rd., Bridgeton. McFerron valued the tower at about $60.

Rain and wind also caused numerous burglar alarms to be set off, county police reported. The alarms caused tie-ups in communications during the peak of the storm, police said.

The police also reported numerous weather-related traffic accidents. No fatalities were reported.

The National Weather Service reported it could not confirm any reports of tornadoes in the area.

A spokesman for the service said winds of 38 miles per hour were recorded at Lambert St. Louis International Airport. He said the damage surveyed so far indicated some of the winds may have reached as high as 70 m.p.h.

ENTERPRISE LEASING
STORMTROOPER

BRENDA KRAEMER

APRIL 4, 1981

The tornado that hit Ladue Road in 1981 was the second major storm to devastate that office. Enterprise volunteers worked all day Saturday to get the office back in working condition for Monday morning. Those volunteers, including Brenda Kraemer (now Brenda Haar) received "Stormtrooper" awards for their efforts.

For an instant everyone froze, then they started to scatter. Two people dashed into the concrete reinforced storage vault and then propped the door open with a book to be sure they didn't get locked inside. Others ducked under their desks, dazed by the sound of the thunderous wind.

The roof ripped open as tree trunks pierced it like arrows, and heavy rain poured in through the swirling dark air. Then there was an eerie quiet, broken only by the sizzling blue flashes of severed power lines.

For a few minutes nobody moved, not yet sure if the funnel was gone. Several of the men started to slog through the water picking up work papers, their pants rolled halfway up to their knees. Most of the damage was from water that had soaked files, and miraculously, no one was hurt. After a quick look around, it was obvious that the combination of downed electrical lines and significant flooding created a dangerous situation inside the building. Police sirens broke the silence, and once the power was turned off, people began to move around. Jack told everyone to leave things as they were. "Let's go outside," he said.

Jack went to his office, took glasses and several bottles from the liquor cabinet he kept stocked for celebrations and special occasions and put them in the back of his car. He led the group to the far edge of the parking lot, away from the tangled trees and dangling electrical wires, and they had the first Enterprise tailgate party, celebrating being alive and safe. The tornado had become one more tie that bound them, and being together for a few drinks took the edge off their shaky nerves.

The next day Busch's Grove (a local restaurant frequented regularly by Enterprise people) invited the entire office over for lunch and offered to store wet files. The phone company forwarded calls from the Ladue Road office to other offices, and the staff scrambled to keep the business going. Rattled nerves were quickly back to normal, and the omen from the skies passed.

No one knew that the energy crisis loomed ominously just over the horizon, but the tornado showed just how Enterprise dealt with a crisis. They stuck together and focused not on the setbacks they encountered, but on the larger goal of survival. The tornado was a harbinger of the harsh winds of change that would shortly blow through Enterprise.

Busch's Grove

SINCE 1890

Busch's Grove

ESTABLISHED IN 1890
9160 CLAYTON ROAD • ST. LOUIS, MISSOURI
314/993-9070

Busch's Grove first opened in 1890 as a stage-coach stop for people going to Jefferson City. It was a friendly fixture in St. Louis, and Jack's father had been a regular patron there when Jack was a boy. Andy's grandmother took him to Busch's Grove for his first "dinner out" when he was a young boy scarcely old enough to sit up straight at the table. Over the years the restaurant became a comfortable home away from home for Enterprise people. For many years management meetings were held in the Pine Room, like this scene with Jack, Johnny Montgomery and Mike Schwarz. Jack regularly conducted business over lunch, and the walls of Busch's Grove have heard all the Enterprise stories, successes as well as failures.

In 1973 the energy crisis caught the entire nation off guard, and its impact was as frightening as an unexpected tornado. Many Americans had become accustomed to unlimited opportunities and resources, and restraint was not the prevailing mood. The sight of President Nixon on television asking Americans to turn off lights unsettled people across the country, and the question of whether or not to put up Christmas lights became an issue of patriotism over personal belief.

Soon there were long lines at gas stations and double-digit interest rates, and uncertainty and anxiety gripped consumers. The car business was confronted with problems it had never known before as gasoline became scarce and expensive. Some companies failed to survive, and others, like Enterprise, held their breath, took measured risks and made it.

Jack knew that he was taking the long view rather than reacting to near-term pressure in his approach to weathering the energy crisis. Many years earlier he had watched automobile dealers create short-term solutions that came back to haunt them, and he had been determined to avoid that temptation. His intuition about the business had served him well, and he had never taken more risk than the company could tolerate.

When Enterprise opened in 1957, customers were eager to buy or lease high-end luxury cars. In 1973, as the energy crisis began, the scene was quite different. Gas rationing drew cars into the stations on even-numbered days for those with even-numbered last digits on their license plates, and on odd-numbered days for those with odd-numbered digits. Even with this rationing, long lines snaked out of gas stations and around street corners, and the pictures of tired drivers waiting in line filled the newspapers and the evening TV news. Anxiety became contagious, and owners of gas guzzlers realized their cars had little resale value.

Enterprise's leasing business reflected the public's attitude. Leasing customers wanted out of the Oldsmobiles and Buicks and into four-cylinder cars that used less gas and were much more economical to operate. Even people who were not so concerned about the cost of gas shifted to smaller cars in order to take on a more acceptable look — anyone behind the wheel of a gas guzzler might be labeled an energy glutton.

As leases matured, Enterprise customers shifted from the bigger cars into the smaller cars, and some customers even terminated leases early just to get out of the bigger cars. Cars like the Maverick, the Pinto and the Gremlin became instant hits. Consumers eagerly bought and leased these smaller cars as fast as they came off the assembly lines.

This quick change in leasing habits

As the energy crisis brought countless cars and people to a standstill, or at least to a slow crawl, gasoline pumps frequently carried distressing signs. The handwritten sign on the pump was a reminder that regular gas, which was the least expensive, sold out first, and people then had to buy the more expensive premium gas until that was gone too.

85

was difficult for Enterprise to handle, but the real disaster was the virtual collapse of the used car market. Enterprise sold to wholesalers the cars it got back from customers at the end of their leases. Wholesale prices had plummeted for eight-cylinder cars, most of which did not get good gas mileage. (There was a limited supply of fuel-efficient used cars, and the ones that were available sold for top dollar.) With resale values declining rapidly, wholesalers did not want to be left holding big cars nobody wanted, so they immediately and drastically lowered the prices they would pay Enterprise. They were eager to either get the cars at a real bargain from hard-pressed sellers in hopes of a sure-fire profit, or at the very least, not take a loss themselves on the resale of the gas guzzlers.

The successful sale of the used car at the end of the lease made possible the profit for the lease, and the inability to sell those cars at reasonable prices as they came back from the customers had an immediate financial impact and dug into the company's reserves. Ray Covington was a veteran manager of car sales at Enterprise by the time the entire industry was overwhelmed by the disarray in the market, and

there was no way for Covington and his managers to predict when sales would pick up. All of the forecasts were bleak, and the long daily gas lines ratcheted up the anxiety level across the country.

Throughout 1974 the only whole-salers interested in big used cars were vultures looking for a cheap deal. The wholesalers who had traditionally bought cars from Enterprise were invisible — they were flooded with cars themselves. It was a "don't call us, we'll call you" time with the whole-salers, and the Enterprise cars sat on the lot with no takers willing to pay a reasonable price.

Jack was the rudder that kept Enterprise on course throughout those stormy days, making clear to his managers his strong feeling that the market would come back and prices would rebound. He saw that the pre-vailing prices for the bigger used cars amounted to exaggerated discounts. Without hesitating, Jack said over and over, "We'll weather this storm." Then he would talk quietly with his financial man, Warren Knaup, and with his car sales manager, Ray Covington, about how long they could survive with their large fleet of unwanted cars.

Day by day the company's inventory

of used cars grew in St. Louis and in other cities as customers' leases ended and the cars came back to Enterprise. The Enterprise office on Ladue Road was surrounded by acres of Ford Country Squire station wagons, Oldsmobile Toronados and other high-end, fuel-inefficient cars that had previously been the cars of choice for the carriage-trade leasing business. The gas guzzlers sat on the Enterprise lot all through the winter, giving the place the look of an abandoned army base full of heavy equipment. They were a constant reminder that the world had become unpredictable.

On those rare times when Jack was alone with no one around, his mind sometimes drifted toward concern about whether he was taking too large a bet — what if he were wrong? What if the used car market got worse instead of better? What if they couldn't lease or rent the big cars still in the fleet? What if interest rates went even higher and they couldn't afford to finance the fleet of big cars sitting idle on Enterprise's lot?

Deep down he believed these fears were unfounded, and he didn't allow himself to get introspective and second-guess his decisions — the fighter pilot mentality kept him focused on

The Oldsmobile 98 Holiday Coupe, left, was a beauty to look at but a beast when it came to gas. It, and other big cars like it, sucked up gas like thirsty nomads gulping down water on a dry desert. The short supply of gasoline and the huge demands of the gas guzzlers created gasoline gridlock throughout the streets of St. Louis and elsewhere, below, as people tried to make the best of a dreary situation.

𝒯his aerial view of Clayton shows the proximity of downtown St. Louis with the arch in the distance. Clayton has been the home of Enterprise from the beginning, and the company's modern headquarters is not far from the office complex on Ladue Road that was Enterprise headquarters for many years. Even today, the home base of the company remains comfortably situated on the edge of downtown Clayton.

getting through the mission. He met almost daily with Knaup and Covington to review the facts and make sure that the risk was not becoming too large. In carefully measured words, Knaup regularly reported to Jack that they could still afford to hold the cars, and Covington reminded Jack that the cars were worth far more than the prevailing prices. Jack was the pilot and Knaup and Covington were the navigators as they made their way through dark skies.

A year later the crisis subsided. Ray Covington had kept his finger on the pulse of the market throughout the crisis and said to Jack, "I think the energy crisis is about over." After months and months when no one was interested in Enterprise's used cars, a wholesaler from Tennessee came to St. Louis buying cars. He told Jack that he had enough confidence to put his money behind this theory, and he wanted to look at what Enterprise had for sale.

Jack and Ray watched closely as the Tennesseean walked across the Enterprise lot examining row after row of cars. Jack had told him he was not interested in selling at distressed prices

*A*fter the first energy crisis, the midsize cars became the most popular vehicles in the Enterprise fleet. Jack and Doug Brown, as well as the entire Enterprise management team, were able to smile again and relax when gas once more became available at relatively inexpensive prices.

— he would only consider reasonable prices for the cars. The man walked back and forth through the lot, then he started marking his best offers with a bar of soap on the windshields of the big cars. Each time he marked a price, Jack felt a growing sense of relief that the crisis was over. He did not argue or negotiate with the Tennesseean because the prices were fair. In fact, Jack respected the man for being an entrepreneur who was willing to take some risks before it was clearly apparent that the crisis was over.

Once those cars were shipped to Tennessee, the logjam broke and other wholesalers started buying again at

prices that were close to fair value. By 1975 the consumer mood had shifted again, and big cars lost their stigma. The big used cars sold at a steady clip as a sense of relief seeped back into the consumer mood.

Jack's long-term view had avoided the catastrophic fire sale prices that could have hobbled the company. Jack, Warren Knaup, Ray Covington, Doug Brown and the other senior managers knew that if the market had not come back, the long-term effect on the company could have been painful. The cost of financing those cars would have eaten away much more of the company's capital and sapped its financial strength.

Jack had faith that the economy would come back. "It won't stay this way forever," he had said frequently with a confident chuckle. He was right. By holding the big cars, the company avoided what would have been a severe multimillion dollar hit for a young company. Because of its history of frugal spending and saving its capital, the company had the financial cushion to make it through the nation's most critical financial crisis since World War II.

89

NECESSITY
Breeds Creativity

By the late 1970s, when the second round of the energy crisis occurred, Enterprise rental managers had become resourceful in finding ways to get around the problem of limited gasoline. Some offices had installed gasoline facilities for their own fleets and were prepared for shortages. In one location, managers fashioned a system where they took the big Oldsmobiles in for gas on whichever days were permitted. Then, back on their own lot, they pumped the gas out of the big cars and into smaller cars. They built a jury-rigged pump system that looked like a modified Erector set so they could stick a hose in the Oldsmobile and then fill several thirsty small cars. It worked, and they kept their rental business alive and growing.

Lines at gas stations slowly disappeared as gas became readily available again and consumers regained their confidence. But the pendulum began to swing the other way. Now it was the smaller cars that began to lose resale value as drivers wanted to get back into something roomier, and the mid-size cars came into their own. Wholesale prices rose quickly as demand picked up again for the big, eight-cylinder cars that could carry the whole family with room to spare.

During the energy crisis, Jack had overseen the diversification of the company's fleet. Enterprise bought Gremlins, Pintos, Novas and other small cars in order to have popular, efficient cars for their customers. (The Gremlin was often referred to as the "tennis shoe," partly because it was shaped something like a shoe, and partly because its snug size made it more like something to wear than something to drive.) Because Enterprise now had a mixed fleet of big and small cars, orderly disposition of the fleet resumed in a way that avoided losses as leased and rental cars became ready for resale. Prices of big cars rose and offset any declines in the prices of other cars. Now Enterprise was able to sell selectively based on which cars were selling best at any particular time. The line-up of big cars quickly disappeared from the lot in front of the building in Clayton.

From that point forward, the company maintained a balance of cars in its rental fleet to assure that it always had enough adequately depreciated cars so that it could sell some cars at a profit to cushion the impact of holding other cars. Throughout the remainder of the decade, Enterprise invested in compact cars, such as the Bobcat, Chevette and Citation, in addition to the larger cars that were back in demand. The fleet became a portfolio of cars similar to a diversified mutual fund where one could look for a good overall return without having too much concentration in one category.

For the first time since World War II, unpredictable events from countries far away from American soil had a quick and dramatic impact on the economy of the United States. Consumers were hit in the pocketbook, and their preferences for cars changed instantly. Never again would the car business be a monolithic and often slow-to-respond industry. The legacy of the energy crisis was the

Prior to the second energy crisis in the late 1970s, the car business was very strong. Compact cars, like the Gremlin, below, had an established market as the public became more concerned about fuel efficiency. Midsize cars also became increasingly popular with Enterprise's leasing and rental customers, left. Many midsize cars still had V8 engines, but as emissions controls were instituted, the distinct sulfur smell of those controls was a reminder the the good old days of carefree gas guzzling were over.

awareness that flexibility and attentiveness to the customers' desires would be the critical factors for success.

If the energy crisis made the car companies more sensitive to the need for flexibility, it also made many consumers more flexible and open-minded in their approach to leasing and rental. Just as customers had been eager to exit the big cars, they were equally eager to enter the small cars, and leasing could make that a quick and easy option.

Many new customers leased small cars because they did not want to end up owning the wrong car. It took the energy crisis for some people to realize that leasing was a good option — if they ended up with the wrong car, they simply turned it in at the end of the lease and somebody else took on the risk of resale. The proliferation of

two- and three-car families by the mid-1970s also contributed to the popularity of leasing. Good economic times and working spouses made it both possible and necessary to have more transportation, and it was transportation rather than car ownership that became the driving concern. Leasing was an inexpensive and flexible way to gain access to another car.

The energy crisis had brought out the best in the Enterprise team as Jack's leadership and intuition about risk saw the company through this turbulent time of change. Rather than just hunker down and wait for the problems to pass, problems became opportunities as Jack looked past

current circumstances and took a longer view. Enterprise emerged from the energy crisis with well-honed corporate skills for solving problems — skills that would be critical to the rapid growth that lay just around the corner. It would be several years before Enterprise would find the business formula for national expansion, but those years would be filled with an array of challenges — a proving ground for emerging leadership.

Assembly line consumer products were a new world for Enterprise. Shifting from a service business into a manufacturing and packaging business with Keefe Coffee called for a different way of thinking. The customer service focus would stay the same, but the customer and the product were now far removed from the company. Opposite: In-room coffee was a business that was in its early stages when Jack bought Keefe Coffee in 1974. The product seemed uncomplicated — bags of coffee — and the ever-expanding number of hotel and motel rooms seemed like a large potential market.

$\mathscr{P}$REPARING FOR THE FUTURE

In 1974 the energy crisis was subsiding, but its ripple effect in the used car market was still being felt. Consumers were edgy about making long-term commitments, and Jack began to wonder if the bright prospects for the leasing business might dim. In the back of his mind, he thought that if for some reason the car business became volatile or unreliable, it might be a good strategy to have a hedge in another business.

Keefe Coffee proved to be a reasonable first step in exploring the pluses and minuses of diversification. The company marketed in-room coffee service for hotels and motels, providing a small, quick-heat hot water heater that was attached to the wall, along with instant coffee. Jack knew the owners, and when one of them suggested that he take a look at the company, he did. In analyzing the business, he asked himself (and a few others) if many people would want fresh coffee in their rooms without having to call room service or walk to the restaurant. It seemed probable to Jack that people would appreciate the convenience, and it was not a terribly complicated business. So he bought it. Jack's interest in Keefe Coffee was piqued by his entrepreneurial belief that something worthwhile could be made of that little company, if only they ran it right. But most of all, it would be fun, it would provide new career opportunities for his people and it would be a toe in the water in another business.

The first person to experience Keefe as a new and different career opportunity was Andy Taylor. Andy had spent most of his school years in various part-time jobs at Enterprise, but when Jack bought Keefe Coffee, Andy had been working full time at Enterprise for only a year. He had worked his way up from his first position as a salesman to become a valuable troubleshooter working closely with top managers in various capacities. He was learning the business from the bottom to the top, but he had not yet held a management position.

Andy thought Jack had gone off his rocker when he said he was buying a coffee company. "Then I *really* thought he was crazy when he asked me to run it," said Andy.

Andy was not the only one who thought that buying Keefe Coffee was a bizarre idea; the accountants and lawyers had recommended that Jack pass on the deal. Flying in the face of informed opposition was a gutsy move, and Andy's focus had been on seeing the leasing business work — not on a new coffee venture. The only thing Andy knew about coffee was how to fix his own, and he had never had full responsibility for a business.

"Look at it this way," said Jack. "It's a great way to get a chance to run a business." Andy agreed.

When Jack bought Keefe, its sales were a very modest $20,000 a month, hardly enough to compare to the automotive revenues. Its customer base was mostly Mom and Pop motels scattered across the country. Andy began analyzing the potential for the coffee company and quickly realized that with the right marketing effort, the business could grow substantially. He began to envision

The one-cup-serving package of coffee was manufactured to make it easy to stock hotel rooms. Housekeeping personnel could stock their carts with coffee next to the soap and towels. Ease of delivery of the product was as important to satisfying the hotels as the right price was.

94

As more and more travelers — business people as well as vacationers — became used to the availability of that first quick cup of coffee in the morning, the in-room coffee business became increasingly competitive. With more competition and greater expectations by hotel and motel guests, the quality of the product became increasingly important. Taste and aroma were new customer service requirements, not unlike the expectations of car customers for clean floor mats and empty ash trays.

EXHIBIT C

PROMISSORY NOTE

$21,428.57
_____, 1974
(Insert Date of Closing)

FOR VALUE RECEIVED, JACK KEEFE COFFEE-BAR SALES CO., INC., a Missouri corporation (hereinafter called the "Company"), promises to pay to the order of TONY HENSCHEL, at the Company's office in St. Louis, Missouri, the principal sum of $21,428.57 with interest from the date hereof on the unpaid balance outstanding from time to time at the rate of 8% per annum.

The principal amount hereof shall be due and payable in nine (9) installments as follows:

Due Date of Installment	Amount of Installment	
	Principal	Interest
Two (2) years from the date hereof	$ 230.61	$3,428.57
Three (3) years from the date hereof	2,649.74	1,695.8_
Four (4) years from the date hereof	2,649.74	
Five (5) years from the date hereof	2,649.74	
Six (6) years from the date hereof	2,649.74	
Seven (7) years from the date hereof	2,649.74	
Eight (8) years from the date hereof	2,649.74	
Nine (9) years from the date hereof	2,649.74	
Ten (10) years from the date hereof	2,649.78	

Interest shall be due and payable (as accrued on t___ pal balance) in installments as set forth above, concur___ installments of principal hereunder.

The Company reserves the right to prepay this Note ___ part at any time and from time to time without premium o___ without prior notice to or the consent of the holder.

This Note is issued pursuant to an Agreement dated ___ 15, 1974, between the Company, Executive Leasing Company ___ other persons and entities who were shareholders of the ___ time of the execution of said Agreement, and is subject t___ right to set off obligations of the payee hereof to the C___ such Agreement against the amounts payable hereunder.

If any installment of principal or interest on this ___ paid when due and payable, the entire amount of principal ___ unpaid hereon shall, at the option of the holder hereof, b___ payable after ten (10) days written notice, sent by certif___ tered mail with postage prepaid, to the Company (c/o Execu___ Company, 8844 Ladue Road, St. Louis, Missouri 63124, Atten___ Taylor), or to such other address as has been theretofore ___ writing to the holder hereof by the Company. If suit is c___ the obligation evidenced by this Note, the Company shall pa___ reasonable attorney's fees in connection therewith.

The Company and all present and future guarantors and endorsers of this Note severally waive diligence, demand, presentment, notice of non-payment and protest, and all other notices in connection with the issuance, delivery, payment or collection of this Note and assent to extensions of time for payment, surrender or forebearance, or other indulgence, all without notice.

JACK KEEFE COFFEE-BAR SALES CO., INC.

(SEAL)

By_____
                        President

Attest:

Nancy C Kraus
                Secretary

*T*he purchase of Keefe Coffee was the first venture outside the car business by the Enterprise management team. Keefe was a small, local business, and Jack was initially concerned about limiting both the financial risk and the management drain it might require from his own staff. His purchase of Keefe was done with a 10-year promissory note to the existing Keefe stockholders, a small group of people in St. Louis and in the years following, Keefe broadened its product line and expanded its customer base to include correctional institutions across the country.

JACK KEEFE COFFEE BAR SALES CO.   No. 30290

"Dedicated to serving you better."

Phone Area Code (314) 968-3636

St. Louis, Missouri 63144

2914 South Brentwood Blvd.

Ship To

Sold To

Road Prison #31
P. O. Box 188
Loxahatchee, Fla.   33470
ATTN: W. L. Gardner

TERMS: NET 30 DAYS — PREPAID ON 150 LBS.

SALESMAN

SHIP VIA	UPS		INVOICE DATE	HH	
YOUR ORDER NO.	DATE RECEIVED	DATE WANTED	B.O. TO S.O. NO.	1/06/76	PRICE	AMOUNT

QUAN. ORDERED	QUAN. SHIPPED	DESCRIPTION	PRICE	AMOUNT
			34.50	$69.00
	2	Cases Individual Coffee	14.75	29.50
	2	Cases Coffee Mate	14.50	14.50
	1	Case Sugar		$113.00

DO NOT RETURN ANY MERCHANDISE WITHOUT OUR CONSENT. DAMAGES IN TRANSIT MUST BE ADJUSTED WITH CARRIER.
NO DEDUCTIONS ALLOWED WITHOUT AUTHORITY.

Thank you for your Business

SHOP OFFICE COPY

Holiday Inn and other fast-growing chains as the right type of customer to foster Keefe's growth.

Andy ran Keefe for several months and then brought Doug Albrecht in from a rental branch to manage it. Albrecht had quickly caught the eye of senior managers at Enterprise because he had a strong determination to master the details of the rental business. He had originally taken a job at Enterprise shortly before he got married so that he would not be embarrassed about not having a job at his wedding reception. He planned to stay at Enterprise only until he could get a "real" job. But the challenge of the rental business and the Enterprise philosophy appealed to him, and his short stint turned into a life-long career.

Andy spent a day or two each week with Doug, working closely with him to define the operating details of buying instant coffee, formulate marketing plans and begin to develop a long-range strategy. Doug settled into the coffee business very successfully and over the next 20 years managed Keefe and other non-automotive businesses Enterprise subsequently acquired, building what is now known as the Enterprise Capital Group — a $200 million-a-year revenue generator.

In those few months, focusing on the big picture as well as the details at Keefe Coffee, Andy had learned what often takes years (or an MBA) to understand — what makes a business successful. Because the focus at Keefe Coffee was on customer service, like the rental business, Andy returned to the car business in 1975 as a wiser manager.

Andy's Early Years

When Andy turned 16 and got his driver's license, Jack quickly immersed him in the business. His first work was doing "repo missions" with Jack, going out at night to repossess cars from customers who had not made their payments. Jack took repos seriously, feeling that a customer who didn't make payments had let him down personally. (Maybe his childhood experience when someone came to get a check or take the car from his father during dinner got his emotions stirred up about repossessions.)

When they went looking for cars, Andy drove the chase car (the car that followed), and Jack took the extra set of keys to bring back the repossessed car. Often the spare keys didn't work — the copies of the early double-sided keys were the worst — and Jack and Andy fumbled in the dark trying to open locked cars. They weren't the types you'd expect to find hustling cars in the middle of the night. Jack never mastered the "tough guy" look, and super-straight Andy in his best khakis and button-down shirts looked more like a high school sports star than a car jockey searching for repos in the dark alleys of St. Louis. If his homework suffered, his intrigue with the car business flourished during those late night cloak-and-dagger adventures with Jack.

One particularly dark night, Andy went with Jack to the house of a customer who was a private detective. As they tried to find the right key to open the car, the man, who had not made his payments, came outside and said quietly, "I have a gun." Jack took one step back and began talking like a snake charmer while Andy leaned against his dad's dark green Porsche, shifting nervously from foot to foot. Finally the man decided not to pull the gun and gave Jack the car, and Andy drove away with cold sweat running down his neatly shaved face.

The leasing business grew steadily during Andy's high school years. Jack frequently brought home a map of

When Andy was in high school, he preferred cars, sports and his friends to his schoolbooks. In addition to his school activities both inside and outside the classroom, he worked during summer vacations at Enterprise. From the beginning he wanted to be treated no differently from any other Enterprise employee, notwithstanding the fact that he was the boss's son.

98

*A*ndy was a
versatile athlete and
played both tennis
and football during
his high school years. As a sophomore wearing number 33,
Andy Taylor was one of the best place kickers in the area.
After his final game as a sophomore, Andy was asked by the
varsity coach to suit up again to play a varsity game with
an archrival later that day. After his sophomore year he
played linebacker as number 66, and in his senior year
the team was undefeated.

Andy met Barbara Broadhurst while at college in Denver, and the two were married in California less than a year later. They spent the first three years of their married life in San Francisco, where Barbara finished school and Andy broadened his business experience in the car business. When it came time to settle down and raise a family, they headed back to St. Louis.

St. Louis, which he updated with colored pins to show the location of every car in the leasing fleet. Mary Ann, Andy and Jo Ann were fascinated as the map got thicker and thicker with pins, none of them ever suspecting that one day there would be a map of the United States covered with a forest of pins. Andy's respect for his father grew, not only because of his nerves of steel repossessing cars in the night, but also because of his success as the owner of a fast-growing business.

During his summers in high school, Andy worked at the downtown St. Louis rental office in the old Lindburg Cadillac building. He (like other new employees) was a glorified porter in a coat and tie. He gave rides to well-heeled customers who brought their Cadillacs in for service, put gas in cars and screwed on license plates.

In addition to his entry-level activities, Andy ran the service follow-up system for reminding the dealership's Cadillac customers about periodic maintenance. Being around people and working with cars beat hanging around the library. Like Jack years earlier, Andy figured out that having fun mattered, and hoped one day to have a career doing what he enjoyed. By the time he finished high school, Andy was hooked on the car business.

Andy's mother saw to it that he toed the line in meeting her and Jack's expectations of what was reasonable behavior for a teenage boy with access to a hot car and boundless energy. She put rules in place, and she made clear that Andy was expected to act according to those rules. One of the rules was to be home by midnight (unless he was out repossessing cars with Jack), and the curfew was enforced — coming home five minutes past midnight resulted in being grounded. Andy particularly resented the curfew. He became a popular guy with his friends, especially in a new 1966 Mustang with spinner hub caps. But the curfew held tight, and when he missed it, the car was parked for several days.

As a senior in high school, Andy applied to the University of Denver and was accepted. After his summers working at Lindburg Cadillac, he knew that he wanted to bypass studying liberal arts and get a business degree as fast as possible. He reasoned that if he went to Denver and got a business degree, he could go to work for a car company, maybe even the family business.

He enrolled at Denver in the fall of 1966 and avoided foreign languages and other subjects that had never interested him. He went immediately into the undergraduate business program for four years of courses that he thought were more practical. His grades were average, not great, but definitely better than the F's his father got in college.

Jack paid for Andy's tuition, room and board, and Andy worked every summer and Christmas vacation to earn his spending money. (His goal was to earn $600 each summer to see him through the year.) He worked in the downtown rental office with Doug Brown and Don Ross, and he learned in detail how the rental and leasing business worked.

Andy was sensitive about being the boss's son and was determined to be accepted in his own right. He did the dirtiest cleanup jobs, such as scrubbing filthy cars, to prove that being the boss's son gave him no advantages. He supplemented his work in the rental office by doing repos on a bounty basis, leaving home at 3:00 a.m. and tracking down as many cars as he could by 8:00 a.m. when the office opened. The thrill of repossessing cars in the middle of the night offset the routine of filling out rental contracts.

One of the mechanics Andy saw almost daily called Andy "the brave," meaning son of the chief. Every time Andy heard that, his back stiffened.

While the mechanic thought it was a clever name, Andy hated being reminded that he was in fact the chief's son. There was no escaping that fact, however, so Andy never said anything. All he could do was work harder. With sheer determination, he turned his resentment toward what the mechanic said into an effort to prove even more clearly that he could handle any job that had to be done, son of the chief or not.

Football and tennis were the focus of Andy's high school life, and classroom work was a chore. In college he balanced academics with sports and his social life better than he had done in high school. At Denver he felt a sense of purpose once he entered the business degree program. Fraternity parties and intramural sports were his diversion from academic work. He had inherited a frugal streak from his parents and he spent his hard-earned money carefully.

FAMILY LIFE AND FULL-TIME WORK

In the fall of his senior year, Andy met Barbara Broadhurst at a fraternity party (Andy was the social chairman of the fraternity), and he fell instantly in love. Barbara was the daughter of a

three-star air force general and had lived all over the world. Their romance took off fast, and for what was probably the only time in his life, Andy put aside his inclination to construct a long-term plan and responded totally to his emotions. He asked Barbara to marry him. She agreed, and the following August of 1970 they married at March Air Force Base in Riverside, California.

During the previous summer (after his junior year in college), Andy had worked in San Francisco with Jack's brother, Paul. Paul managed a large

By the mid-1970s Andy and Barbara had moved back to St. Louis. Kelly, above, was their first daughter. Neither Andy nor Barbara could have known then his future success as a businessman.

Lincoln-Mercury dealership that also had a rental and leasing business associated with it. Andy loved being away from home, but he looked like a misfit in California in the 1960s — his hair was as short as a Marine's, and over-the-counter cold medicine was the strongest drug he knew. His parents' discipline during his early years had become a part of him, and he had no interest in drugs or a hippie phase.

That visit to San Francisco had whetted his appetite for being away from home, so after he and Barbara married, they moved to San Francisco. Barbara was two years younger than Andy, and she had one year of college to finish. She went to school at the University of San Francisco, and Andy worked downtown with Paul and Paul's partner, Leroy Hardwicke.

At first they rented an apartment in Daly City in a subdivision that had been an artichoke farm not long before. After a year they bought a small house in a middle-class neighborhood in Marin County and Andy commuted into the city every day over the Golden Gate Bridge. Their life was simple and happy — Andy worked long hours, Barbara studied at night, and on weekends they relaxed. They played tennis and wandered through Golden Gate

Park. They ate in simple restaurants and spent much of those evenings just talking. (One favorite place was an Italian restaurant with long tables, food served family style and wine in tall soda bottles that were refilled whenever empty.)

Andy spent three years working with Paul in San Francisco. He learned the ropes of customer service by dealing with any customer who walked in the office — even the cranks. He also had frequent phone conversations with Jack. Jack was both father and mentor for Andy, listening patiently to the customer problems Andy was handling and providing guidance for the tough situations. Executive Leasing was growing steadily, both in St. Louis and out of town, and Jack shared with Andy the successes that were taking place at Executive.

By late 1972 the thrill of being in California had worn thin. Andy and Barbara enjoyed living in San Francisco, but Andy was feeling restless about his future and was beginning to miss his Midwestern roots. Their first child, Kelly, was born in San Francisco, and Andy felt the urge to settle down.

He had done well in his work — he was proud to be making over $20,000 a year to support a family, and he played

the role of the "front-line" problem-solver in Paul's business. What had once been the strong satisfaction of being the unflappable problem-solver had turned into a constant frustration.

One morning Andy looked in the mirror and said, "This isn't fun any more." That same day Jack called just to catch up on things, but the conversation quickly turned to Andy's future. "Why don't you come on back here," was how Jack put it, giving Andy no more details than Arthur Lindburg had provided when he hired Jack.

Andy and Barbara moved to St. Louis on a dreary winter day in December 1972. Andy and Jack sat down to work out the details of Andy's new position. From the beginning they called each other "Jack" and "Andy," making clear to themselves and to others that their relationship in the office was a business relationship. Jack wanted to be certain that Andy was treated the same as any other new employee; for starters that meant a large pay cut. What had been a good income in California was cut by a third. But that was part of the company culture — if you wanted the job you had to be

102

willing to sacrifice to make it work.

Andy and Barbara had thought that the cost of living would be lower in St. Louis and that their money would go further. They sold their house in California for $48,000 (a profit of $5,000 over what they had paid for it) but soon found that would not buy a very large house in St. Louis. They did find a house, and though it was not the home of their dreams, it was only 20 minutes from the office. With a baby at home and the usual pattern of long hours at the office, Andy appreciated being close to home.

Barbara had not been excited about the move to St. Louis. For her, San Francisco was a wonderful place to live, full of interesting cultural opportunities, and she could envision having a family there. However, once they did decide to move to St. Louis, Barbara was as committed as Andy to making it work. She recognized Andy's dedication to the company and knew that his commitment was different from just having a job. One Tuesday each month, she and other company wives went out to dinner. Those dinners were occasions for fun, not crying on each others' shoulders about their husbands' long hours. That camaraderie forged relationships that grew deeper among the women as the

years passed. Barbara continued to play an active role with other wives in the company, and she became very involved in the community and civic life of St. Louis.

Andy's first full-time job at Enterprise started in January 1973 when he went to work as a salesman leasing cars in the midtown office run by Bill Lortz. He worked on a commission basis, and from the beginning, he had to scramble to find business. He started with no base of business and took inquiries from customers who walked in. Winter was a hard time to lease cars, and by late 1973 the energy crisis created confusion and anxiety for prospective customers.

Late in 1973 Andy went to work with Warren Knaup, learning procedures for the accounting and business activities in Enterprise's out-of-town locations. That work was interrupted when Andy was once again tapped to do damage control. A top salesman who leased 300 cars a year had been fired for not treating customers properly, and Andy was thrown back into the leasing business.

Andy became the firefighter. He was glad he had learned to scramble around in California placating customers and handling numerous tasks at the same time. He also realized that he was

comfortable working within the structured environment of Enterprise and its more methodical approach to solving problems.

By the time the energy crisis became a major factor in doing business, Andy was wearing several hats and spending most of his time close to Jack and the other senior managers. He wrote leases, collected unpaid bills and took Barbara on repossession runs (repossession runs having become something of a family tradition). He had honed his problem-solving skills through on-the-job training, and for the first time, the firefighter role was comfortable because he was genuinely committed to building the company.

February 1974 was the lowest point for the company during the energy crisis. Enterprise lost money that month after writing down the value of some of its used cars. (The company has not lost money in any month since then.) Andy watched Jack as he pulled the team together with the strength of his leadership. Jack was now the mentor for Andy that Arthur Lindburg had once been for Jack, and the crisis became a learning experience.

Then in late 1974 Jack bought Keefe Coffee, and Andy moved from problem-solver to manager.

103

The Houston skyline emerged in the 1970s and 1980s as a symbol of American capitalism charging full speed ahead. Businesses grew, office towers sprouted up and Houston would never be the same again. It was an important place to be for any company that expected to have a nationwide presence. Opposite: This "Everyday Man" was a frequently featured character in Enterprise advertising in the 1980s.

$\mathcal{I}$NTO THE BIG CITIES

Enterprise's expansion into top-tier cities nationwide came partly by chance and partly by deliberate planning. By 1974 it was clear that the St. Louis way of doing things worked elsewhere. Atlanta was profitable under Bill Lortz's new management, and the Florida operations were all doing far better than anybody had ever guessed possible.

The next step in Enterprise's expansion was making the commitment to move into the big cities, but it was a step Jack had always been reluctant to take. His concern was practical — "the competition there could eat us alive," he said whenever the possibility of moving into a top-tier city was discussed. The closest Enterprise had come to a top-tier city was a small, struggling leasing office in greater Houston. This 1973 foray into Texas was a rough beginning, but by the end of the decade, Enterprise had found a formula for success in the big cities.

In 1973 an opportunity surfaced for Enterprise to establish a presence in Houston, and John Ebeling was the man who was willing to take a chance on opening that city's market for Enterprise. Ebeling's career had started a decade earlier in St. Louis. He was an apprentice mechanic in a foreign-car repair shop, having gone to work after two years of college. He was working 12 hours a day, six days a week, and loved his work, but he knew he didn't want to stay in the shop forever. He was a friend of Doug Brown and had heard great things about Executive Leasing. On Christmas Eve, he met with Bob Mohan, Executive's sales manager. Mohan looked up at the delivery board that tracked the deliveries of leased cars and said, "Your pal Brown is gonna make $800 this month."

After some discussion, Mohan hired Ebeling for $400 a month to be a runner in Executive Leasing's lower-level office at Forest Cadillac. There was no job description, so Ebeling did whatever Mohan needed to have done. He picked up cars from dealerships, picked up license plates, screwed on outside rear-view mirrors, swept the floor and cleared snow off cars all winter.

Bob Mohan was an extraordinary salesman. He had been with Executive since the outset, and many newcomers like Ebeling learned a great deal from him about making deals. Mohan loved sales more than paperwork, and over time, as he drifted further from sales and more into management, his enthusiasm for the business ebbed.

In 1970 Mohan had left Executive to work for a competitor and was running the Houston office of Manchester Leasing. That Houston office was in trouble — it had already been open a few years and was continuing to lose money. The owner of Manchester Leasing called Jack and asked if he was interested in buying his Houston operation.

Just prior to going to lunch with the head of Manchester Leasing, Jack called a meeting with his branch managers and said that unless one of the branch managers was interested in going to Houston, he would cancel the lunch. John Ebeling raised his hand and said, "I'll look at it, Jack." Ebeling didn't know exactly where Houston was (he thought it was where Dallas is), but he smelled an opportunity. He had not been in touch with Mohan for many years and had no idea what to expect in Houston. Ebeling, Jack and

Doug Brown flew to Houston, and Ebeling ended up staying.

The problems with Manchester Leasing were substantial: the rental business was full of bad debts, and of the 276 long-term car leases, only 26 were to qualified customers. Jack decided not to buy the office and take on all that bad debt, but he was persuaded by Manchester to work out its problems under a management contract. The advantage of this contract was that it provided a way for Jack to get a closer look at the Texas market without overly committing resources of people or money. He was confident that Ebeling had the skills to work through the Manchester problems, and he felt they could gradually generate new business.

The first office in Houston was in a "temporary" building known as "the zoo." It was a double-wide trailer inherited from Manchester, and by removing the skirt that had been placed around the front edge, you could see where the axles had been. The ceiling was so low that light bulbs could be changed without a ladder. A persistent leak in the roof rotted the floor near Ebeling's desk, and the soft spot under the shag carpet gradually grew larger over the next two years. Andy Jansky

*A*fter the first energy crisis, business boomed for Enterprise in Houston. Lu Galloway and John Ebeling stood by a Monte Carlo, which was the hottest leasing vehicle in 1976. The car looked better than their office, which was known as "the zoo" because of the incredible volume of business that quickly developed at that location.

was the rental manager, and he worked out of a zippered briefcase because there were not enough desks.

From the beginning Ebeling's job was to clean up the problems they inherited from Manchester. John and his wife, Barbara, spent much of their first year in Houston repossessing cars. Barbara was a sleuth who was superb at tracking down leased cars on which payments were delinquent. She was as stealthy as any repo man alive — at all hours of the day and night. One time Barbara's brother Roger came to visit and got pulled into the repo business. John went to bed fairly late but was still surprised the next morning when Barbara informed him, "Roger and I went to get that truck, but it wasn't there."

"That was just part of the job," Ebeling recounted years later, seated at his desk in the general manager's office in Houston. "We were all in it together, the whole family."

Once the Enterprise team had tackled the task of finding, repossessing and selling over 200 cars, they began to build a new leasing and rental business. As was fast becoming the standard operating procedure at Enterprise, the new office was a combination of enthusiastic local talent and experienced managers promoted from within

the company. Andy Jansky, the rental manager, and Dave Castle, the business manager, came to Houston from St. Louis, and the rest of the team was assembled locally. Some Manchester employees were kept on the payroll, though most didn't measure up to Ebeling's standard. (In fact, the receptionist was taken away by ambulance due to a drug overdose.)

Houston was full of transplants during the mid-1970s, and business-people were judged by what they did rather than where they came from. That environment was conducive to the Enterprise team's hard-working strategy, but they suffered hugely from not having the word-of-mouth support marketing that had been always present in St. Louis. As Ebeling tracked down cars by night and wrote leasing and rental business by day, an added pressure was the success of other Enterprise branches.

While there were questions from St. Louis about the status of their progress, much of the pressure Ebeling felt came from within. He had gone to Houston because of the challenge, and he refused to believe that a winning strategy could not be found. The trial-and-error experiences of Atlanta and Florida were all history now, and while

he wanted to learn from those other experiences, he still felt the gnawing absence of a winning business plan.

At the same time, Ebeling slowly admitted that he was spreading himself too thin. It simply was not possible to roam Houston for repos night after night and then arrive fresh at the office at seven a.m. and be effective with the staff and with prospective customers. Something had to give, but he could not figure out what it should be.

As he was trying to find daylight on any front, Ebeling was hit by the energy crisis. He was known as "the king of Oldsmobile Toronados" — he had more of them than anybody in Houston — and that car had the lowest fuel efficiency of any American-made car. During the energy crisis Ebeling became increasingly desperate to unload these gas guzzlers. He constantly tried to cajole used car dealers into buying a Toronado from him. He had very little luck, and at one point, considered taking the trunk lids off and using the Toronados as flower boxes in front of the zoo.

As the red ink continued to hit the bottom line month by month, Ebeling felt greater pressure to generate more business. While the rental business was growing slowly, Ebeling began writing leases too aggressively, and many of them were bad. He was re-creating the same problem he had gone to Houston to solve. He stayed awake nights, torn between his knowledge that he could make Houston succeed — he knew how to write good leases — and his feeling that he had to deliver new business fast.

During the Christmas holidays in 1974, Ebeling was at a party at Jack's house in St. Louis. He felt both frustration and guilt about not having done better in Houston. Jack took Ebeling aside and gently but clearly told him not to worry about the volume, "Just do it right." Ebeling finished his drink and left, feeling a huge sense of relief and recognizing that Jack had been there before and understood his dilemma.

Ebeling felt that the future of the business was in rentals, so he concentrated on building a rental business and put leasing on the back burner. But it was still slow going, and when Houston had a loss of $15,000 one month, he was worried. Doug Brown, his boss in St. Louis, called and said he was coming down for a visit.

Prior to going to Houston, Brown, Jack and Warren Knaup had lunch at Busch's Grove to talk about closing down Houston. As they discussed the

Warren Knaup, Doug Brown, Andy Taylor and Don Ross (left to right) concentrate on the details of the business at the annual general managers' meeting. Often these annual meetings were held at the Lake of the Ozarks, in part to get away from the office and take a hard look at the business, but also to go somewhere fun. The business side of the meetings focused on policies, procedures and operational details with less attention to big-picture strategies. Through this attention to detail, over the years the larger corporate strategies emerged naturally without having to be forced into place.

tedious process of unwinding the Manchester problems, Jack said, "Doug, it just isn't worth fighting any more. Go close the place and bring Ebeling back to St. Louis."

Brown went to Houston planning to stay for two days and stayed for five. The first night there, he had dinner with Ebeling and told him that Jack was concerned, very concerned, and did Ebeling want to come back to St. Louis? Ebeling said he wanted to stay and make Houston work. Over the remainder of that week, Brown and Ebeling went over every aspect of the business from details of the leasing strategy to details of the expenses. After hearing Ebeling's story, Brown

109

was convinced that Houston could work if it was given more time.

When he returned to St. Louis, Brown met with Jack to report on his Houston trip. "How is John?" Jack asked. Brown replied, "Fine." Jack pushed further: "How did he take it?" To which Brown responded, "I didn't do it. We're not going to close now." Jack was taken aback. "I sent you down there to close the place. Why didn't you do it?"

Brown said that he thought closing down would be a hasty response to a problem that was likely to get better soon. "What is it going to cost us if I'm wrong?" Brown asked Jack. "Not much more." Jack was not patient with

$\mathcal{M}$eetings have always been a vital part of the Enterprise culture. In the earliest days, the meetings involved only Jack and one or two salesmen. Then the Pine Room at Busch's Grove became the customary spot for meetings with a group of a dozen or so managers. When the group grew to include managers from all parts of the company — leasing, rental and general managers — the meetings were broken into smaller groups to better serve their purpose. Managers' meetings at Enterprise have been a way to touch base with Jack's philosophy and for individual managers to keep their eye on the goal. The meetings focus on details, but not just the problems of the day, and they are an important way to share ideas that are working well. They are also a time for fun and staying in touch with friends who have moved on to other locations.

continuing losses, but as in other times, he was willing to take some risk if the financial threat was small enough and his confidence in his managers was great enough. He respected the conviction Brown and Ebeling expressed and gave them a chance to make it work.

Early in 1975 Houston turned the corner and moved into black ink as the rental income increased and the leasing losses decreased. Ebeling was focused solely on new business and was no longer spending nights repossessing cars with his wife. The rental business was growing as the insurance companies got to know Enterprise. Once the bad leases were straightened out, the leasing business also grew steadily. Ebeling was tired, relieved and proud.

In 1976 Ebeling felt that they had at last hit on the right formula. The business in Houston was finally profitable; they even opened a second office. Once it was clear that the short-term profits came from rental and the longer-term profits from well-written leasing business, Ebeling and his staff were ready for a bold move into downtown Houston. There was no more shag carpeting to cover rotted flooring — it was even possible to jump on the floor without risking injury. There were several extra desks

as part of the plan for growth. Growth came much faster than before. The fleet got bigger, and the profits grew. The tough years paid off, and Enterprise was solidly positioned in its first top-tier city.

In 1976 Jack convened his management team and branch managers (a group of about 15 people) in a meeting room in the Clayton Inn Hotel to talk about expanding the business. The rental business was working well, and Jack, with great encouragement from all his managers, expressed his determination to roll the business out nationally. He pulled out some automotive jargon of the day and told the group, "We're going to put the pedal to the metal." That meant moving into the big cities, and setting the company on a fast-growth track that positioned Enterprise as a major national leasing and rental company.

A NEW GAME PLAN FOR DALLAS

The annual unveiling of new car models each fall was a big event, and auto manufacturers staged a dramatic "teaser" campaign to stimulate consumer interest. Cars were gradually unwrapped on television over several weeks, first showing a bumper, then a

tail light and finally the whole car. Every September the Enterprise managers gathered at the Lake of the Ozarks in Missouri to talk about the new model cars and about leasing strategies. Enterprise formulated its leasing plans to coincide with the arrival of new models, so the September meeting was always a big event.

In 1978 about 40 Enterprise managers piled on a bus and rode three hours from St. Louis to the Lake of the Ozarks. The body shop reconfigured an old Trailways bus by taking out a row of seats in the middle of the bus, thus making room for tubs of beer and a supply of sandwiches for the ride. At the meeting they talked about rental and lease rates, depreciation schedules and fleet size — technical details of the business. For fun there was golf, boating and plenty of places to go for dinner.

The gossip during the meeting that year was that Jack was thinking about opening in Dallas. All of the out-of-town locations were doing well, and there was a sense of momentum in the company. Jack did not mention Dallas during the meeting, but others speculated about his plans.

The day after Christmas that year, Doug Brown called John Grimes, then a manager in Atlanta, and asked him if

The Arrival of
RALPH

Once Jack moved the company into the fast lane, it was clear that a new approach was needed to handle the administrative side of the business. With the rapid expansion of the business, manual ledger sheets were everywhere and the monthly computer printouts from the service bureau were too little and too late.

Marc Cohn was working at IBM in St. Louis when Jack first met him in 1973. Cohn was well settled with a good job in a big company, was in his 30s and was not looking for a change. Jack was struck by Cohn's curiosity about how business strategy worked and how technology could allow the development of new strategies, not just crunch numbers faster.

After a few general conversations, Jack offered Cohn the job of coming to Enterprise and building a system of technology to support the business. Cohn

In 1982 the data processing department was Marc Cohn, Doris Kester, Ann Dabler, Ray Sadowski and Mary Drowzkowski. The computer room was at 35 Hunter Avenue, and the machine was a System 38, IBM Model 5. It had one megabyte of operating memory and 1.2 gigabytes of total disk storage. Today Enterprise uses equipment with approximately 3,000 times as much storage capacity as was available in the early 1980s.

112

Roger Price and Jan Massarella started the national reservation department in 1982. Their job was to handle reservations for people who needed a car outside of their home city, often businesspeople traveling or vacationers who wanted a car for a short-term rental. The national reservation system now has over 375 employees and operates 24 hours a day, every day of the year. Every year these Enterprise employees handle over seven million incoming calls dealing with reservations, roadside assistance and insurance replacement vehicles in the U.S., Canada and the United Kingdom.

was unsure. Jack then said to Cohn, "I guess it's a question of whether you believe in IBM or whether you believe in yourself." Cohn took the job and only later realized that at the time of his move, the total revenues of Enterprise were less than the bad debts of IBM.

Cohn immersed himself in the company, learning how the business operated before deciding it was time to buy the first big computer to run accounting functions for the St. Louis headquarters. Cohn sponsored a naming contest for the computer in an effort to get businesspeople comfortable with what was, for most, their first computer. One of Cohn's employees, Warren Burghardt, proposed that the computer be called RALPH, standing for "rapid and logical paper handler." RALPH it was, and Enterprise was on the road to the modern world of technology.

On a Saturday in 1974 there was a companywide "conversion party" to transcribe the leasing accounting information from the old format to the new format for the computer. Everybody from mechanics and car washers to senior managers showed up to get the massive amount of data moved to the new system.

Carmen Davis worked in accounting, and she got the job of "sweeping up after the parade." Once the conversion party was over, the tedious task of identifying and fixing the glitches was Carmen's role. First she tackled the obvious discrepancies where dollar amounts were clearly wrong. Then she moved on to the tougher problems where parts of the system needed adjustment to make the work flow smoothly. Within a month the computer was running smoothly and the old system was history.

Everyone got used to RALPH, at least until a leasing salesman was hired whose name was Ralph. The salesman was quickly dubbed "the real Ralph," though the computer was fast becoming a real part of the lives of Enterprise people throughout the company. As the expansion effort continued through the years, Cohn kept pace by adding new capabilities to RALPH. Not long after accounting, a program was developed for leasing calculations.

The big technology leap occurred when rental managers saw how RALPH had improved business and became believers that technology could push their businesses to new heights.

The introduction of the rental business to the computer system became the launch pad for the current Enterprise system. Enterprise has become a technological giant. In 1996 construction began in St. Louis on the Enterprise Technology Center, which was designed to manage the world's largest IBM AS/400 host configuration of equipment, a network that connects 26,000 terminals throughout the Enterprise world.

Exceeding Expectations

By the time John Grimes and his team established the Enterprise presence in Dallas, the company was becoming increasingly capable of playing to its strengths in new markets. Imposing skylines no longer seemed intimidating. Now they were viewed as chock-full of rental prospects. The insurance replacement business continued to be a rock-solid foundation for growth, and Enterprise worked hard to make clear the benefits it had to offer to insurance companies and their adjusters.

115

he wanted to move to Dallas and open an office. Grimes had lived in Dallas briefly some years earlier but was now settled comfortably with his family in Atlanta. That night he took his family to dinner at a Red Lobster restaurant and laid out the proposition. His wife, Ellen, agreed that it was a great opportunity, while his two sons wanted to know about the sports programs there.

Once the decision was made to move, Grimes announced to his family on the morning of New Year's Day 1979 that they were all going to watch the Cotton Bowl Parade to see their new city and to get into the Texas spirit. Dallas was immobilized that day by an ice and snow storm, and the parade looked like an adventure from the far Yukon. A few weeks later, when Ellen Grimes arrived in Dallas to look for a house, another ice storm hit. Dallas's reception to the Enterprise family was frigid — at least on the weather front.

John Grimes arrived in Dallas on February 12, 1979, and went to the office space that Enterprise had rented for him. There was a strong wind blowing dust everywhere. The office was an old Quonset hut which had previously been home to an auto parts business that had stopped paying rent. Several window panes were broken, and there were dead bugs on the moldy carpet when Grimes went inside. The concrete interior was painted black, red and white — a far cry from the Atlanta office full of Southern charm that he had left behind. He found one rotary phone that had a dial tone, and since the lights didn't work, he stood by a small window to get a streetlight shining on the phone so he could dial. He called Ellen, who was still in Atlanta. "How is the office?" she asked. His reply was, "Honey, it's not Atlanta."

Stan Mann had moved from St. Louis to Dallas as the rental manager, and that move gave Grimes the necessary talent to get the business started. But nobody in Dallas had ever heard of Enterprise, so hiring locally was a very slow process. The scarcity of trained people was a growing concern throughout Enterprise. Very soon the prices of gasoline started to rise, and the Texas economy slowed down. The downturn in the economy made it easier to hire people in Dallas — any job was better than no job, even if it meant working for an unknown company from St. Louis. Grimes and Mann were fortunate in attracting strong local talent — Tom McKinley, Kevin Neary, Dave Nestor, Jeff Gardner, Mark Harris, Tony McKinnis, Jacques Juneau and Scott Kendrick all were early members of the Dallas team who through the years moved on into senior management jobs in other Enterprise locations.

The business strategy in Dallas was clear from the outset — lead with rental. The economic environment meant that many companies in Dallas were watching costs closely. Enterprise was not interested in establishing fleets of leased cars, so the company decided that emphasis on daily rentals was the right strategy for that market at that time. The goal was to generate profits fast, and the daily rental business turns a profit more quickly than long-term leases. For the first time the Enterprise strategy was to have a large impact fast and build a critical mass of business. Up until then expansion had been a slow process of opening one office at a time and waiting for each to become profitable before starting the next one.

The accuracy of this strategy was demonstrated by Enterprise's swift success in Dallas. The first office was officially opened a few weeks after Grimes arrived. A second office was opened two months later and then a third office three months after the second. The daily rental business did generate profits quickly, and the Dallas operation was in the black in 1981. The tough economy also drove out many marginal competitors who could only survive when times were good.

The pick-up-and-delivery plan that had worked well in Florida was transplanted to Texas and set Enterprise apart from any other local competitor. John Grimes and Stan Mann drove cars all over Dallas, sometimes going from East Dallas to Arlington, a distance of 30 miles, to deliver a car. One would drive the car, and the other would follow to pick him up. The aggressive, competitive style of Enterprise worked well and was successful in getting business. Within two years Enterprise had six offices in Dallas, and the rental business was even more successful than expected.

While John Ebeling had spent his early days in Houston repossessing leased cars, John Grimes was on the road in Dallas delivering rental cars. The five years between Houston in 1974 and Dallas in 1979 had been a turning point for Enterprise. Daily rental was now the lead business, and it was clear that it was the entry ticket into the big cities. The dark days of the energy crisis were now in the distant past, and the success of the national expansion effort was unquestioned.

The movement into Houston and Dallas had fashioned a formula for strategic expansion that would be critical for the success of future expansion — lead with rental, build a quick critical mass of offices, let leasing grow naturally. Ebeling and Grimes had supplied the ingredients others would use for their later successes.

This brochure underscores the way in which Enterprise led with the rental business in the expansion into Dallas. It stresses convenience, service and the company's specialized experience with insurance replacement rentals — qualities that customers appreciate, as the numerous locations listed at the bottom confirm.

Announcing our new rental location

ENTERPRISE
RENT-A-CAR
Division of Enterprise Leasing

RICHARDSON
525 W. Arapaho Rd. #11
IN NORTHRICH CENTER
½ MILE WEST OF CENTRAL EXPWY.
234-1581

- One call service
- Primary liability, comp and collision to drivers 25-65
- Free pick up and return
- Professionalism based on 25 years specializing in insurance rentals

Other Convenient Locations:

DALLAS NORTH/3210 Beltline Rd. #124/214-620-7997
DALLAS NORTHEAST/11844 N.W. Hwy./214-328-9126
DALLAS DOWNTOWN/2600 Cedar Springs/214-742-7087
IRVING/1305 W. Airport Freeway/214-258-8050
ARLINGTON/201 West Division/817-265-5424
HURST/8011 Grapevine Highway/817-485-6363
FT. WORTH/2733 West 6th Street/817-332-5900

MEXICAN INN
BRAND
CHILI WITH BEANS

NOTHING TO ADD • FULLY COOKED

SERVING
SUGGESTION

IN CONVENIENT OVEN-PROOF T

NET WT. 14 OZ.

MEXICAN INN CHILI PRODUCTS, INC. • ST. L

The Mexican Inn story was a difficult but important chapter of Enterprise history. No one likes the taste of failure, particularly the hard-charging Enterprise team that is used to earning its successes one at a time by hard work and focusing on the goal. Mexican Inn taught Enterprise managers that they are not invincible, and that they cannot be all things for all people. It also taught them that they are capable of learning new businesses. Opposite: The Mexican Inn name has become part of the Enterprise vocabulary and is used as a watchword against ventures that don't fit well with Enterprise's strengths.

$\mathcal{A}$ BITTER TASTE OF FAILURE

"Don't give me a Mexican Inn" was an admonition Andy used throughout the 1980s. That phrase had its origins in a defining experience in Enterprise's history. The company ventured into the Mexican food business, suffered a large loss and learned a painful lesson about the portability of certain Enterprise business philosophies. Enterprise had come to feel invincible — all of its expansion efforts were succeeding, the company was growing rapidly and the energy crisis was a distant memory. It seemed as though Enterprise's breadth of talented, seasoned managers could succeed in any business. Failure was new, unexplored territory, and when it hit, it hit hard.

In the mid-1970s the acquisition of Keefe Coffee had been a successful venture for Enterprise due to Jack's vision and Andy and Doug Albrecht's successful management. The business had grown, its customer base was now stronger and more diverse and its philosophy was rooted in a commitment to customer service. As a result of the success with Keefe, the Enterprise Capital Group was formed to acquire and manage small businesses that had significant growth potential.

Success was not to be found in the case of Mexican Inn Chili Products, makers of institutional Mexican food products for schools and restaurants. Mexican Inn was a St. Louis-based company that was small, wanted to grow and found its way to Enterprise. The human factor was persuasive since the owner was known to Enterprise.

After considerable internal debate, the decision was made to buy Mexican Inn Chili Products in 1977. Once it was part of the Enterprise fold, Enterprise was called upon to invest substantial capital in the company to create a retail line of food products. As the retail products came to market, Enterprise found itself on thin ice — it had no knowledge of packaged goods, nor did it understand competition in

the food business.

Enterprise's success was based on having direct contact with its customers and having control over the way in which the relationship evolved with individual customers. The retail Mexican food products were sold through food brokers to customers the company never saw face to face, unless the Enterprise managers happened to wander down the aisles of the local grocery stores.

What had initially looked like an interesting entrepreneurial opportunity turned into a deal that went from bad to worse as the venture moved into its second and third years. The products did not sell, and Enterprise could not figure out why. Finally sales picked up, and there was a huge sense of relief.

Unfortunately, the relief was short-lived and quickly produced heartburn for Enterprise. Mexican Inn had sold the Mexican food products to retailers on a guaranteed buyback basis, so when the retailers could not sell the products, they returned them to the company. Suddenly the oversupply of Mexican Inn products was reminiscent of the glut of gas guzzlers that had haunted the company a few years earlier. It was as though retailers had borrowed the products to fill their shelves, and when

they didn't sell quickly, the retailers returned them. Something was badly awry at Mexican Inn.

Apart from not understanding consumer patterns for buying Mexican food products, Enterprise failed to recognize the cultural misfit with the people in the acquired company. Mexican Inn was so strongly imbued with the roll-of-the-dice style of doing business that it simply could not fit within the Enterprise system of taking measured risks. At Enterprise there was a clear but cautious willingness to experiment with risk, while the mentality at Mexican Inn involved a constant flirting with danger. If a plan worked, it worked well. But if a plan failed, the result was disastrous.

During 1980 Andy spent a great deal of time with Jack trying to figure out what to do with Mexican Inn. (Andy's job then was running the car business in the St. Louis group, but he had moved closer and closer to Jack as the Mexican Inn problem became more critical.) Andy took his concerns to someone removed from the situation — Doug Albrecht. After analyzing the business carefully, Andy and Doug were convinced that the time had come for the company to cut its losses and move on. Andy had also put a lot of effort into being sensitive to the people involved, trying to soothe the inevitable bruises of a bad situation.

After a bad case of corporate indigestion, Andy knew it was time to make a hard decision. After further analysis of the financial impact and after more conversations with the various people involved, Andy told Jack that he felt it was time to get out of the business. He felt that, if anything, they had waited too long to face reality.

"The first loss is the best loss," he told Jack. "We missed the opportunity to cut our losses early, and now is the time to do it." Jack agreed. The efforts to turn the business around had been lengthy and had required a large time commitment from both Jack and Andy, as well as Doug Albrecht and others involved in trying to salvage the business. It was time to move on. He felt that Andy had made a tough decision

fairly, and his own intuition about the Mexican Inn dilemma told him that it was a sound decision.

"You're right," Jack said to Andy. "Let's get on with it. It's time to focus on our own business and be done with this."

Andy was tremendously relieved to hear Jack agree. He was eager to get rid of Mexican Inn Chili Products and get back to the basics of the car business.

Then Jack added, "And I want you to be the president of Enterprise."

Andy, then 33 years old, was, for once, unprepared. His mind got tripped up by his feelings, and he couldn't say anything. Then he blurted out "Wow," and it sounded

louder than he meant it to sound. "Thanks," Andy said with a wide grin. Putting to rest Andy's previous insecurities about being the boss's son, Jack replied, "You've earned it."

The Taylor team was moving on, slightly older and considerably wiser after its foray into Mexican foods.

The Mexican Inn experience did not scare Enterprise away from new ventures. Non-automotive acquisitions continued throughout the 1980s and 1990s, and drawing on earlier experiences, the company has made other acquisitions successful. The Enterprise Capital Group has grown to over 650 employees and consists of numerous companies located in different parts of the United States.

As Enterprise grew across the country, the company became more sophisticated in its approach to the business. It kept focusing its attention on details and paid close attention to the characteristics of an increasingly diverse customer base. California became an important piece of the expansion puzzle as Enterprise moved to new heights of growth during the 1980s. Opposite: The acquisition of the AirCar rental system was the beginning of operations for the Enterprise rental business in California. The AirCar acquisition was a marriage of the Enterprise management style and the Californians' dependence on "wheels."

$\mathcal{T}$HE RIGHT PEOPLE AND THE RIGHT STRATEGY

123

During the early 1980s the company's expansion continued its steady advance across new frontiers. The efforts in Houston and Dallas had become a foundation for strategic growth. While it had become clear that Enterprise could go into a new market and clean up the problems created by others, it was also clear that a market focus on rental was the right route to take in building new business.

The company had also learned to balance its intuitive insights about the business with hard analytical homework. The combination of a clear-cut strategy and a balanced style of management put the emphasis on the key Enterprise ingredient for success: the people.

"What are you doing?" Bill Holekamp asked the guard at the newly acquired rental office in Los Angeles one day in 1980.

"I'm guarding the cars," was his reply. He held up the notebook in which he logged cars in and out for that day in 1980 and nodded casually over his shoulder toward the fleet of cars parked behind the chain link fence.

"Why are you doing that?" Holekamp persisted. "The neighborhood doesn't look so bad."

"It's not the neighborhood," the guard responded with a cynical smile. "It's the employees. Some of these people take a car home for lunch, walk back to work, then we're short a car."

Something did not compute in Holekamp's logical brain. He and a team of a dozen Enterprise managers had just completed a long, complex negotiation to acquire a rental business in Southern California. They had cautiously structured a deal that was intended to limit the risk Enterprise would take in buying the troubled car rental business.

And then he learned that the employees had been stealing cars. Holekamp scratched his head and said, "Well, we've got to put a stop to that." The guard looked up and laughed cynically, adding, "Good luck."

The wheels for the acquisition had been set in motion early in 1980. Paul Taylor (who was still working in San Francisco) learned that a Ford dealer in Los Angeles was having problems and was interested in selling a rental business, known as AirCar, that was part of the dealership. The dealer was a man Paul knew and considered a reputable guy.

A sluggish economy had slowed the car business in Southern California, and this dealer was hit particularly hard. Demand for his Ford Pintos plummeted when the design problem with the Pinto gas tank became a national consumer issue. (Some of the Pintos had exploded on impact, and this dealer was hit hard because he had a large inventory of Pintos.) The final straw was that some of the film studios to whom he had rented cars failed to pay their bills.

When Jack sent the Enterprise team to Los Angeles to study the condition of AirCar, his marching orders were clear. "If you find anything there that we can fix and use, let's do it. If you can't find anything we can fix, let's not do it."

There was a sense of momentum at Enterprise when the call came from Paul to look at Los Angeles. The expansion efforts in Atlanta, Kansas City and Florida were now paying off as those locations generated steady income for the company. Houston had turned the corner and was profitable. Dallas was just getting underway, relying primarily on the rental business. The rental fleet continued to grow, both in St. Louis and in the out-of-town locations.

Jack liked California. He had traveled there regularly with Arthur Lindburg years earlier, and more recently he had stayed in touch with Paul and the business he was doing in San Francisco. The confidence he felt from the earlier Enterprise expansion efforts buoyed his enthusiasm until someone would refer to the state as "granola land," and he would wonder if the California culture really was that different. Would the Midwestern ethic work in Southern California? Were the customers different? Was the business formula different?

People in California were "car crazy" — committed to their cars in a way that was unique to California, and

The California Enterprise team was led by Bill Holekamp, center. Dave Willey, on the left, who had worked for Holekamp in St. Louis, moved to California and became a rental manager in Los Angeles. Ira Robb, on the right, had been part of the AirCar management team when Enterprise acquired the company, and Robb played a crucial role in building the highly successful marketing effort in Southern California. Robb succeeded Holekamp as general manager of the Southern California group when Holekamp returned to St. Louis some years later. This rate card explains that Enterprise initially operated AirCar's Southern California locations as a separate division.

most particularly to Los Angeles. People spent hours on the freeways commuting to work in the sprawling city. They thought nothing of driving an hour to do an errand, and they rarely had access to public transportation. The clever "vanity" license plates started in California, creating a personality for both the car and driver. The Enterprise people from St. Louis quickly saw in Southern California a serious commitment to an automobile lifestyle that they had never seen anywhere else.

Because of the distances they drove and the general lack of public transportation, being grounded without a car had a serious impact on all aspects

of life in California, from making a living to buying groceries. People simply had to have a car.

As a result of this reliance on automobiles, the car rental business had developed earlier in California than elsewhere. Many car dealerships had rental operations, and replacement vehicles were a big business. Enterprise quickly found that it did not have to educate consumers about the need for a rental but instead had to concentrate on providing rentals efficiently.

Once the acquisition of AirCar had been completed, Jack asked Bill Holekamp to run it. Holekamp had gone to high school with Andy and had worked his way through the Enterprise ranks. He started on the finance and accounting side of the business and became exceptionally proficient in managing the operating functions of the company. His structured and organized approach to business gave Jack a feeling of comfort as they moved into the unknown world of the car business in Southern California.

As Holekamp headed west, Jack told him that he had full confidence in him. In order to fix the inherited problems and to start building new business, Holekamp asked for additional working capital. "I'll put in another $500,000 to get it running, but that's it," Jack responded. Jack had clearly limited the risk of this new venture, and Holekamp went into it with his eyes open.

Holekamp convened the staff of AirCar and began explaining how business would be different. The Enterprise way of doing business meant that customer service was the top priority. Employee integrity was essential. Men wore coats and ties to work, and women wore suits or dresses.

One employee raised his hand and said he did not have a suit or jacket, but he did have a sweater vest that he had worn to his sister's wedding. Would that be okay? No. Buy a jacket.

What did he mean by integrity, someone else asked? We won't be locking the gas pumps and picking up the cash from every branch every night. We have to trust you, so make sure you don't take what isn't yours.

Could you explain customer service? Everybody in the branch is responsible for anything and everything that has to be done. People behind the counter wash cars and pick up customers. You do what it takes to satisfy the customer. That answer produced some shifting around as AirCar employees experienced the Enterprise culture shock.

Holekamp concentrated on correcting operating problems at the same time that he was instilling the Enterprise sales and marketing mentality. The administrative work at AirCar had been done by the accounting group of the dealership that owned the company. Enterprise people started looking at the accounting and business procedures in order to get full control over the operations of the business.

As they examined how work was

being done, they discovered a shoe box full of American Express and Diners Club credit card vouchers totaling nearly $100,000 and close to four months old. The AirCar person who was in charge of billing customers was asked about the shoe box. "When we get in these credit card slips from the branches, we match them with the rental contracts. Sometimes the numbers don't match, so we set them aside. That's what these are. We just got behind and haven't had a chance to trace these."

That was one of the few easy problems to fix. The vouchers were deposited in the bank that same day, and the research was done regularly thereafter to keep them current.

By 1980 problem solving was an established part of the Enterprise management style. Whether it involved operational problems like those of Houston or Los Angeles, or customer service problems that occurred every day throughout the company, the approach was the same: fix it once, and fix it right.

The sales and marketing work in California was a challenge as it became clear that people there had different expectations than people in the Midwest or Southeast. In California

MBA'S CAN WASH CARS
As Well as Manage

Bill Holekamp first worked at Enterprise during his high school years — he knew Jack because Bill and Andy were school friends, and Jack asked Bill if he needed a summer job. Bill worked in the Clayton rental office for Wayne Kaufman at a time when that office had 50 rental cars. Holekamp was the guy who did whatever was needed, washing cars or calling "George," his contact at Missouri Credit, when new customers came in to find out if they were a good credit risk.

After college Holekamp went to business school and graduated from the Wharton School of Finance with an MBA in Management Information and Control. After getting his graduate degree, he talked with an investment banker he knew about his future. Holekamp described his interest in small, entrepreneurial businesses, and his banker friend introduced him to Roger Penske, who had just purchased a leasing company in Pennsylvania, a company that leased cars as well as heavy-duty trucks.

After two and a half years with Penske, Holekamp returned to St. Louis in a marketing role with Boise Cascade. The marketing role was a new challenge to build on the finance and administrative skills he had been developing, and the job got him back to St. Louis. Holekamp became the "orange juice king" in charge of frozen concentrate containers at Boise Cascade and continued in the marketing role there for several years.

Holekamp had continued to stay in touch with both Andy and Jack, and Jack said to him in 1976, "Quit wasting your time with those big companies and come to work where you belong." Holekamp had been around the business world long enough to have seen that the Enterprise philosophy was truly unique. The only promise Jack made was that the company was growing and that if Holekamp were any good, he could be part of it. And that promise rang true.

The company did grow, and Holekamp, like other new employees, washed cars in addition to his work in finance and marketing. He increasingly broadened his experience into the broad array of skills that would be essential for the move into California. He learned management and business skills both in the classroom at Wharton and on the job at Enterprise.

Even though Bill Holekamp had a long-time connection to Enterprise (he went to school with Andy Taylor), an MBA and an established career in marketing, he got down and dirty with the rest of the new Enterprise employees when he came aboard in 1976. His multi-faceted experience was perfect training for his role in the company's expansion into Southern California.

Throughout the 1980s all the Enterprise general managers went to St. Louis in December for a meeting and party. As long as the management group could still fit in Jack's house, the holiday party was held there. At this party, above, Andy and Paul Taylor listened to stories from Bill Holekamp about his adventurous early experiences in California.

As the company continued to grow by leaps and bounds, Jack maintained a balance between working hard and relaxing. He was never far removed from the business, and relaxation was an important ingredient in his lifestyle. He maintained the coat and tie at work, but quickly shed it when it came time to relax. Jack married Susan Orrison in St. Louis on July 27, 1979, and at this costume party, above right, he seems very relaxed indeed, though he did not win the prize for best costume.

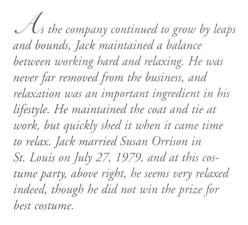

there was a strong interest in foreign cars well before Enterprise had added a large component of foreign cars to its overall fleet. In line with Enterprise's commitment to customer service, the company determined that if that was what people wanted to drive, that was what Enterprise would offer. The fleet mix was changed.

The diversity of the population was also unlike other parts of the country. There were huge numbers of immigrants moving into California constantly, and Enterprise had never before dealt with people who spoke different languages or came from foreign cultures. Hispanics, Vietnamese and Koreans were all potential customers whom Enterprise had not encountered in the past.

Ira Robb had worked in the car rental business in Southern California for 20 years when Enterprise bought AirCar. (Part of that time he had worked at AirCar.) He was 38 years old, had never lived in St. Louis and had never worked for a rapidly expanding national company. But what he did have was an intuitive sense of the market in Southern California — he had street smarts.

After some uncertainty on both sides, he went to work for Bill Holekamp. They were an unusual combination — the rational thinker and the savvy salesman — but it worked. Enterprise employees called them "The Odd Couple." However, what they shared was a fierce determination to succeed, and together they created a base of skills and a management style that no other rental company in California could equal.

Meanwhile, Holekamp was very aware that he was using up his $500,000 of working capital at a steady rate. In the first few months he decided to clean house and get rid of all the problems he could find, both uncollected receivables and unreliable employees. That housecleaning was expensive, and the early losses

were much greater than even he had expected. He had taken a significant pay cut when he moved to Los Angeles, as was usual when a manager got a promotion to run a new area. The butterflies in his stomach never showed in front of the employees, though when he got edgy and testy, some of them wondered how long Enterprise would hold on with the losses mounting.

"You never lose until you quit," Holekamp's grandfather had told him, and he never quit.

The first two years were very hard. Even after a substantial housecleaning, it took a while to put aside all the problems from the past. It also took longer than expected to hire and train the staff — the competition for good employees was stiff since Enterprise was not a well-known name in

As Andy's role in the company grew during the 1980s, he and Jack developed a close working relationship. Each has respect for the other and they have been able to disagree without injuring their relationship. Andy began calling Jack by his first name when he returned to St. Louis from San Francisco. It was common practice for Enterprise employees to call Jack by his first name, and it was more comfortable for both Jack and Andy than "Dad." It acknowledged their professional working relationship, but never diminished their close personal tie.

and the losses diminished gradually. Holekamp knew that the success was the result of all the parts fitting together — rental, customer service, used car sales and getting rid of the inherited problems. There were many small breakthroughs until the red ink turned to black, and then a huge sense of relief that together the team had made it.

As the Enterprise business in California grew throughout the 1980s, Holekamp kept shifting his sights higher and learning about how to succeed in the Southern California market. The issue of how far apart branches should be located demonstrated the need to break free of preconceptions.

In Los Angeles, it became clear that branches could be very close and complement each other rather than compete with each other. Holekamp had nearly closed a branch in Beverly Hills because it was only 15 minutes from the Westwood branch. Conventional thinking was that locations should be farther apart, but the breakthrough now was that more branches closer together would create a synergistic result of more business for everybody.

The Enterprise locations that Bill Holekamp, Ira Robb and their team nurtured in Southern California grew into a formidable presence, attracting huge numbers of new customers as they built the business office by office. At the outset the Southern California business had 60 employees and 800 cars. Nearly two decades later the business has grown to approximately 1,800 employees and a total fleet of over 42,000 cars for rental and lease customers.

status-conscious Southern California.

Holekamp used $450,000 of the $500,000 Jack had promised as working capital before the business turned profitable. The upturn came slowly, as the cost of the problems faded and the revenue from new business grew. But each month business got a little better,

Holekamp hired Enterprise's first recruiter in order to staff the fast-growing rental business. Prior to the arrival of the recruiter, hiring had been done by rental managers as part of their job, and employees were found through employment agencies. They simply could not hire enough people this way, so the California Enterprise group turned to the recruiter in spite of considerable internal skepticism. Even more skepticism crept in when they started hiring recent college graduates. The notion that kids right out of college didn't know anything and could not be relied on was quickly proved false by the energetic and dedicated performance of these recruits, and Enterprise in California grew even more rapidly.

The California venture started on shaky feet. Careful nurturing made the feet steady and the foundation strong. After 12 years there were 150 offices in California and over 20,000 rental cars. The expectations about how much business could be done in one area had been changed forever. California had also been a frontier for Enterprise in discovering that there were no identifiable limits to how much business a well-trained, hard-working Enterprise team could generate.

CALIFORNIA DREAMS
Come True

Pam Nicholson is just one example of how promotion at Enterprise works. Pam, a management trainee in a St. Louis rental branch, volunteered to move to California, seeking a better opportunity in a new growth area. After more than a decade of experience building the Enterprise reputation in California, she was appointed vice president/general manager of the New York group.

Pam Nicholson was working behind a rental counter in St. Louis as a management trainee when the first jobs began to open up in California. She was eager to move — her husband had a job offer in California, and she saw potential for fast movement for herself as Enterprise moved into this new market. She voiced her desire to go to California as a management assistant, and she got the job.

Nicholson went to work in a rental branch in Orange County. "We focused on replacement rental business," she recalls, "and we worked hard to get a foot in the door." California had been open about a year when Nicholson arrived, and the marketing effort was still in the early stages. The entire branch staff, which included both men and women, concentrated on going out and marketing to the dealerships, insurance companies and body shops to make Enterprise known to them and to seek business.

At that time no one had heard of Enterprise in California, and the competition was intense. Nicholson and others worked hard to sell the benefits of Enterprise customer service: "I never doubted being able to sell Enterprise, either to insurance agents or to mechanics in body shops. We all were confident of what we had to sell, and it worked."

Nicholson worked in California for 12 years, moving up through the ranks from management assistant to regional vice president. When she left California in 1994, the Orange County region had 22 offices and a fleet of 3,500 cars. In 1996, after two years in a corporate role in St. Louis, Nicholson was promoted to manage the New York group. The 12 years of experience in California, coupled with her drive and determination, moved her into the senior ranks of Enterprise managers, where she manages over 1,000 people and hundreds of offices.

132

Enterprise's first Chicago office, which opened in 1983, combined the best aspects of Enterprise expansion efforts to date. Bob Klaskin led a small team of Enterprise people assembled from across the country to seize the opportunity they all saw in this big city. Taking measured risks, the Chicago team built a fleet of 15,000 vehicles by the mid-1990s.

Putting it All Together in Chicago

Bob Klaskin's asthma kept him out of the army. He took a job at Enterprise after interviewing with Doug Brown and Jack because "I had a blind faith in myself," as he describes his feelings at the time. In 1967 he started in the daily rental business in midtown St. Louis as branch manager, along with Bob Bell and Don Ross in the leasing department. The team of three young guys tried to figure out how to rent cars, since there was not a definite game plan at that time for the rental business.

After three years and a successful track record, Klaskin accepted an offer to become a used car salesman at the Enterprise office on South Kingshighway, where he again would join up

with Don Ross, who was the branch manager there. When he told his wife, Marilyn, she had visions of plaid coats and plastic white shoes and asked if she would have to tell her friends about his new job.

But there was no shame in it for Klaskin. Like many of his buddies at Enterprise, his faith in himself propelled him forward. The mere scent of

a challenge would draw Klaskin and others into the fray. By this time the Atlanta office had opened, and the possibility of future opportunities in other out-of-town locations was an additional motivation.

Like his earlier jobs, that job went well for Klaskin, and he later moved into a leasing job. Seeing other managers such as Don Ross make

out-of-town moves as opportunities expanded, Bob and Marilyn talked about the possibility of a move elsewhere. She supported his eagerness to look for significant opportunities and told him she would go anywhere he wanted to go — except Florida.

In February 1974, as the winter winds howled in St. Louis, Klaskin learned about an opening in Tampa for a branch manager. Late one night in bed with the lights out, Klaskin said to Marilyn, "Guess what. There's a job in Florida I want." The lights came back on, and the two of them sat up most of the night talking about Florida.

Klaskin went to Tampa having no idea what to expect. The energy crisis was painful in Florida — keeping gas tanks full required wasting valuable time in long gas lines. The Thunderbird went from being the hottest car in Florida in 1973 to the coldest in 1975 as its gas-thirsty V-8 engine became a drawback instead of a symbol of power. Managing the fleet was as difficult in Florida as it was in St. Louis.

Difficult times taught Klaskin and team members like Bill Lafferty valuable lessons about fleet management that would stay with them throughout their careers. Klaskin and his team in Tampa worked aggressively with insurance companies to build new rental business based on replacement cars. By the time he left Tampa in 1983, Klaskin was a 16-year veteran Enterprise manager who had had his hands in all parts of the business. And he had worked successfully outside of St. Louis.

In 1983 Klaskin knew that expansion into Chicago was a hot topic within the company. He and Marilyn decided to visit Chicago on their own to see the city. He said nothing to anyone at Enterprise, flew to Chicago from Tampa and rented a Budget car. They spent four days driving around Chicago. As they were about to head back to the airport for the flight to Tampa on Sunday afternoon, they looked at each other and said, "We could do this."

That visit made Klaskin see Chicago as a huge opportunity. He saw positives rather than negatives: 10 percent unemployment meant that 90 percent of nearly 8 million people had jobs. To Klaskin, the city was full of average Americans who would need rental cars to get to work.

Klaskin returned to Florida and volunteered to move to Chicago. Andy agreed that Klaskin was the right manager to open Chicago, so in August 1983 Bob and Marilyn Klaskin moved from Tampa to Chicago, where it was 105 degrees (far hotter than the summer weather in Tampa).

The first Chicago office was in an abandoned firehouse in Elmhurst. (The city had built a new firehouse and sold the old one to Enterprise through a bidding process.) The building had two long garages, and in the back there was a kitchen and locker room.

Klaskin and Doug Brown found the building the way Enterprise managers usually find new locations — getting out on the roads and driving around, watching traffic patterns and looking for locations near the car dealerships.

During the few months it took to purchase the firehouse from the city, Klaskin scrambled to get ready for business. He assembled a team by hiring some experienced Enterprise people. One manager was hired from Enterprise in Kansas City and two more rental people were brought on board from Enterprise Houston. Klaskin accumulated leasing and rental supplies at home since there was no office in which to store them.

On September 28, 1983, he met the other members of his newly formed team on the front steps of the firehouse. (He knew the manager from Kansas City, Bruce Kruenegel, but had only had telephone conversations with Christy Ratchie and Janet Sobolak, the two managers whom he had hired from the Houston office.)

The four members of the Chicago team shook hands and started unloading supplies from the back of Bob Klaskin's car. The next day the first customer showed up as the unpacking continued. This customer had been referred by the dealer from whom Klaskin had purchased the office's first cars.

"Are you a rent-a-car company?" the customer asked with some hesitation as he gazed at the stacks of boxes where fire engines used to park.

The logical response was to say, "No, we're not open yet." But years of conditioning caused Klaskin to respond immediately to the customer's need. "Sure, how can we help you?" Some quick rummaging through boxes produced a rental contract and a ballpoint pen. Shortly thereafter the customer left in an Oldsmobile Cutlass Supreme, and Enterprise was in business in the Windy City.

A few months later the second office opened. It was December, and the temperature hit 28 degrees below zero with a wind chill factor of 82 degrees below zero. Between August and December Bob and Marilyn Klaskin experienced a temperature swing of 133 degrees in their first year back in the Midwest.

But by December it was clear to Klaskin that the opportunity he had initially seen intuitively was in fact there. The strategy of leading with rental was working, and the team was performing at a high standard. "I felt

like a self-employed man," he said. "We took risks, we made things happen. Nobody did it for us." Klaskin's track record meant that the risks he took in Chicago were carefully measured risks. He fit the profile for taking on a top-tier city.

The goal in Klaskin's mind when he arrived in Chicago was to achieve a rental fleet of 2,500 cars over a number of years. That would be a threefold increase over Tampa and seemed logical for Klaskin in a bigger market. During the first year, when the expected losses occurred, Klaskin was encouraged by Andy to stick with the program.

"If you want to open more offices, let's do it," Andy told him. "Then when it turns profitable, it will be even stronger."

Others were just as eager as Klaskin had been to head a new office. Young rental representatives Rick Allen and Phil Hernandez saw their opportunity and moved their young families from Kansas City to Chicago in the dead of winter in order to help Enterprise establish a stronger presence in Chicago.

By the time Klaskin was building the Enterprise network in Chicago, it was clear that the basic Enterprise game plan of aggressively building the rental business and letting leasing

follow worked well. It had been tested during the 1960s and 1970s in warm weather and cold weather, smaller cities and now bigger cities, and the strategy produced strong results.

Klaskin knew what his results were each month, and when the initial losses occurred, instead of pressure, he received support, both from the top down and from the bottom up. Most of the pressure was generated by himself, by his own determination to show himself and others that Chicago would succeed, but the Chicago team had faith in themselves and in their strategy. They knew their plan was going to work. By the mid-1990s the Chicago fleet totaled 15,000 cars, far exceeding what Klaskin or anyone in St. Louis had initially thought would be possible.

Chicago was the expansion effort that brought all the pieces together, and the success of the Chicago team was fantastic. The Enterprise formula of starting with intuition, adding a well-crafted strategy and engineering the venture with a carefully matched team worked. Enterprise found that with the right business strategy and the right staff, growth was very nearly guaranteed. The game plan would be repeated many times as the Enterprise engine shifted into high gear.

The friendly face of Enterprise spread quickly across the nation throughout the 1980s. The simple routine of picking up customers quickly became a trademark of the Enterprise rental business. Picking up customers brought Enterprise service to the customer's doorstep and built strong, loyal customer relationships. Opposite: This car-covered map titled "Enterprise States of America" represents the company's expansion in the 1980s — growth that covered the nation with Enterprise's cars.

Chapter Eleven

ENTERPRISE GOES NATIONAL

Throughout the 1980s the Enterprise expansion produced staggering results
as offices were opened at a rapid pace in cities all across the country. By
1990 the number of Enterprise offices had grown to more than 800.
During that decade the nationwide rental fleet increased from 6,000 cars
to 100,000 cars. The formula for expansion had been tested and was
working well — lead with rental, build a critical mass of offices quickly
and manage the groups with people who become part of their communities.

137

The growth was east to west and north to south — Philadelphia to Phoenix, Seattle to Sacramento, and Pittsburgh to Portland. Everywhere Enterprise opened offices the demand for rental cars surged to record levels. The underlying question behind this growth was, What did all these people do for rental cars before they rented from Enterprise?

While it seemed that no one explanation could completely answer that question, the reality was that Enterprise was changing the habits of consumers. People who used to catch rides with friends and neighbors increasingly discovered the ease of renting a car, even when theirs was not in the shop. The replacement rental business remained strong, but throughout the country it was clear that much of the growth came from discretionary rentals — when people wanted an extra car for visitors or a different car for a trip or special occasion.

With the evolution of the expansion formula, critical mass of locations became an important driving principle. The lessons that had been learned in California about being able to put offices close to each other without creating competition now rang increasingly true in other locations. Multiple offices in close proximity meant that more people learned about Enterprise from word-of-mouth advertising, and discretionary rentals became convenient. And with more and more offices close by, the repeat business (which Jack had first emphasized in the early days of Executive Leasing) also grew. By the mid-1990s Enterprise was close to the point of having a location within 20 minutes of 90 percent of the people in the United States.

The geographic expansion throughout the 1980s and 1990s focused on the Enterprise style of management — find a manager eager to open in a new part of the country, make that manager feel ownership for that business and provide a safety net to assure that risks are properly managed. Even with hundreds of offices, Enterprise kept its original policy with regard to transfers. When decisions were made to move into new regions, the word went out throughout the company asking which managers were interested in the new jobs. From those who raised their hands, the new manager was picked. No one was ever told they were being transferred. Only volunteers made it to the short list of candidates. Once they got the job, they were told to run it themselves and call when they needed help.

138

As the regional expansion continued, the growth of Enterprise's rental business continued at record rates. The expansion into the Southeast typified what was happening across the country as the Enterprise presence began to blanket the country.

THE SOUTHEAST

"I went for a walk on the beach. I was scared to death. After Doug called and said they wanted me to open in the Carolinas, I knew this was what I wanted more than anything, but now I was scared. What am I going to do, now that I've got the job? I've never managed anything like this before."

After the phone call from Doug Brown, Dick Rush flew from Florida to St. Louis to prepare for his move. The instructions sounded simple: Dick, your group is the Carolinas and part of Georgia. Go up there and find locations, do the leases, order the cars, hire the people and when you need money call us.

Doug Brown took Rush to dinner while he was in St. Louis. After a long, rambling conversation, Rush finally revealed what was on his mind. "When are you going to tell me what to do?" Rush asked Brown. He felt that surely

the time had come when he would be told the secrets of the expansion game plan — what to do, when and how.

Brown's answer to Rush was the same message that went out to numerous Enterprise managers who headed off to the unexplored new territories. "When you have a question, you decide the answer — unless you think the answer could get you fired. If that's the case, call me and we'll talk about it."

Rush commuted from Florida to North Carolina for nearly six

As the national expansion continued, the Enterprise presence covered entire regions. In the early days of expansion, a tentative foothold was established in a new city and gradually branches were added. By the 1980s the formula for opening offices was clearly successful and entire parts of the country were quickly covered, creating an important critical mass of Enterprise offices that could benefit from combined regional marketing efforts.

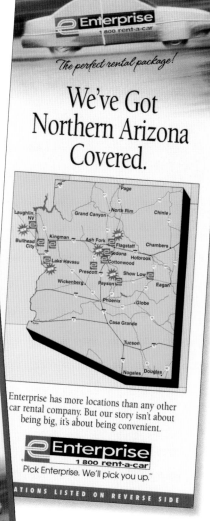

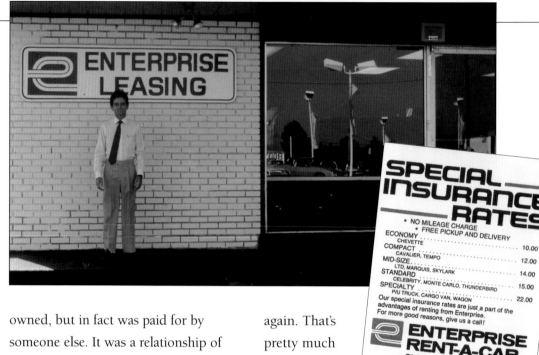

Insurance replacement business was a critical part of Enterprise's national expansion. Enterprise had carefully nurtured relationships with insurance companies and their adjusters from the beginning of its rental business. By the 1980s Enterprise was well known by many insurance companies, and the company's high level of customer service fueled the rapid growth. This, the first office in Columbia, South Carolina, opened in 1988. The rate card was the Charlotte office's first.

months while he looked for the right locations. "I drove around most of the day, first one city, then another. After a few months, you get a feel for the cities. I generally wanted the office to be near the main drag in town, not on it, but just around the corner. I wanted to be convenient, but didn't want to pay the top-dollar rent of dealership row. If you keep driving around and looking and asking questions, you can find the right locations."

As Rush kept searching for the right locations and then began to negotiate the leases, he kept in touch with Brown in St. Louis. Often several weeks passed when they didn't talk at all, then they would have a long conversation to catch up on all aspects of the progress. Brown kept reiterating to Rush that he was to run the business as though he owned it, and Rush understood the responsibility that went with running a business that he felt like he

owned, but in fact was paid for by someone else. It was a relationship of trust on both sides.

In November 1984 Rush opened the Enterprise office in Greensboro with a rental fleet of 15 cars. In December he opened an office in Raleigh, and by then he felt that his months of research driving the streets were beginning to pay off. In January Rush opened the third Southeast office, this one in Charlotte. Once these offices were underway, he began rolling out the rental strategy that had been successful in Orlando.

Rush describes in simple words what he and his people did in the early days: "We came to work, washed a few cars, answered the phone, we rented some cars, we went to pick some people up, we went to lunch, we came back and did the same thing in the afternoon, and then we went home. We came back the next day and did it

again. That's pretty much what we did, and we had a good time doing it." He watched his managers grow increasingly capable, and he began to treat them as he had been treated — run your business, call if there's a big issue.

This management style worked. By 1993 the rental fleet in the Southeast was over 4,000 cars, by 1995 over 8,000 cars and by 1996 over 10,000 cars. (Rush's original goal when he moved from Orlando was to build a fleet of 2,000 cars.)

As a result of this explosive growth, Rush and some of his peers in other parts of the country started a new process of "regionalization." The basic rationale was that if he kept dividing his territory into smaller and smaller pieces (creating sub-regions

140

within the Carolinas and north Georgia), the managers would not be stretched too thinly and would make better decisions. Split, divide and conquer became the new variation on the expansion strategy. The goal was to stay very close to the customers, and to also provide career opportunities for managers who were eager to move onto new challenges.

For Dick Rush, being able to take the Southeast group through its birth and adolescence was the American dream come true. "I feel like I own it, but everybody else here feels like they own it too. That's how I want it to be."

Rush's success signaled future success for Enterprise's regional expansion across the country.

SPREADING THE WORD

One morning in 1988 Jack got out of the shower and watched television while he dressed. As he watched a commercial for one of the car manufacturers, he began wondering whether Enterprise should take a more aggressive stance in the marketplace. He watched other commercials of national companies roll by on the screen, and it occurred to him that it was time for Enterprise to publicize its image of customer service and its practice of picking up customers. Some competitors had started to pick up or deliver rental cars, and his sense was that the first company to tell a particular story got the most impact. He also wondered how he would feel if a competitor beat him to the punch with this story; he might then lose the competitive advantage Enterprise already had established.

Jack talked at length with his friend Bill Claggett, who had had a long and very successful career in corporate advertising. After numerous conversations Jack hired Claggett to help him think through the issues associated with national advertising. Jack's instincts told him it was time to get on with a national advertising campaign, but he wanted to proceed cautiously.

Rental managers were quick to see that high performance was rewarded, both with recognition for past accomplishments and with new job opportunities. The area and city rental managers above show their excellence awards at the annual awards banquet in the Southeast group.

141

LOCATIONS, LOCATIONS, LOCATIONS.

ENTERPRISE RENT-A-CAR

The Special Delivery™ Company

As the expansion gained momentum, the number of rental employees skyrocketed. Meetings, always an important part of the Enterprise culture, continued, but now on a larger scale. The annual rental managers' meeting became an increasingly popular event where city and area rental managers could talk with each other and with Jack and Andy. This meeting took place in Keystone, Colorado, in 1990, at which time Enterprise locations blanketed much of America.

Claggett took Jack to New York to meet with four advertising agencies to discuss the possibilities of an agency relationship with Enterprise. Jack described to the advertising people in New York that this would be his first venture into national advertising, and while Jack wanted to do it right, he wanted to pay close attention to his budget. (True to form, Jack wanted to limit the downside risk in case things did not turn out

as well as expected.)

Three of the four agencies turned Jack down. They seemed to feel that a tight-purse-strings approach was not the right way to start. One of the four, Avrett, Free & Ginsberg, told Jack and Bill Claggett that they would like to work with Enterprise on a proposal for national advertising. Jack returned to St. Louis eager to proceed.

When he talked with Andy about his idea, Andy offered a cautious reaction: "We do need to think carefully

about spending a lot of money on advertising. But we also need to think about the process, how we go about it."

After lengthy discussions about the rationale for full-scale advertising, Andy and Jack decided to proceed. An advertising committee was formed within the company to oversee the process, and Avrett, Free & Ginsberg went to work. They agreed with Andy that research was the essential starting point, and they began the process of analyzing what consumers knew about Enterprise.

The research made clear that picking up customers was the greatest differentiation in consumers' minds between Enterprise and its competitors. They also learned that the customer service emphasis created a "warm and friendly" impression of the company. With this research in hand, the creative process started.

Jack expressed the strong view that the commercials must portray Enterprise employees in a way that would make them proud. "When they watch it, or when their parents see it, I want them to feel good, to feel proud of themselves," Jack instructed the agency. Andy and the internal advertising committee agreed.

"There are better-known car rental companies than Enterprise, but none that know their customers better."

With that line, the first commercials began airing in the fall of 1989. Earlier in 1989 the company's name had been changed from Enterprise Leasing to Enterprise Rent-A-Car to reflect the predominant role of daily rentals. The first advertising campaign focused on the nationwide rental business, but it was intended to create an awareness of the Enterprise name, not to boost rentals immediately.

Within the company the reaction was mixed. One concern was the question of money, not the substance of the commercials. The compensation of Enterprise managers is based on the bottom-line profit of the business, and additional expense eats into the profit. Their concern was practical; some felt that the business was growing well without the added expense of advertising and did not want to feel it in their own pocketbooks.

They were also concerned whether national advertising was necessary, since much of the rental business had been controlled or influenced by local insurance agents and adjusters. Why focus on the individual consumer if it is our relationships with the insurance companies that actually affect the flow of business? But the research indicated

Becoming a
GOOD OLD BOY

Paul Daigle was a native of Louisiana and one of the first employees in the Baton Rouge office, but he experienced culture shock when he moved to the mountains of east Tennessee. While some Enterprise managers were opening offices in the lights of the big cities, Daigle and other Enterprise managers across the country were learning the realities of life in small-town America.

Daigle's job was to get Enterprise established in Knoxville, Tennessee, and then move into the towns of upper east Tennessee. "I'll never forget the first car we rented in Knoxville," recalls Daigle. "Somebody wrecked right in front of our office just after we opened. I went out and made sure nobody was hurt, called the police for them and then rented a car to one of the drivers. I was genuinely concerned about the people and wasn't trying to be an ambulance chaser, but at the same time, I felt

we were right there when they needed us. We didn't have any other customers who came to us like that. The rest of them we had to go find."

Once Knoxville was operating well, Daigle moved to Johnson City, Tennessee, in 1991. Because real estate was tight, his first location was 100 square feet in a dealership and body shop. Daigle had four employees cramped in space that they quickly named "the dungeon." (Even the lower level of Forest Cadillac in 1957 was less cramped than Daigle's first office in upper east Tennessee.)

Daigle learned that in order to find customers he had to get to know insurance adjusters who were used to doing all of their business with local people they had known most of their lives. Change did not come easily when the competition was small local rental companies who had strong ties through-

out the community.

One adjuster confided to Daigle, "This is a good-old-boy network because we all know each other around here. Until you become a good old boy, there just isn't going to be business coming your way."

Daigle's quick reply was, "How do I get to be a good old boy?"

The adjuster looked Daigle straight in the eye and said, "Just keep knocking at that door; it will come through for you."

Daigle and his staff kept knocking on doors, and it did come through. The growth in the small towns of east Tennessee moved at a near-record pace throughout the 1990s. "Our goal is to be number one," says Daigle as he looks toward further expansion. "Every month we strive to be better. Sometimes we have a bad month; that happens. But I can guarantee that we won't have two bad months back-to-back."

that rental decisions were steadily passing to the consumers. Adjusters were now more inclined to suggest several rental companies to their customer and let the customer pick. If the customer was going to make the choice, name awareness was critical.

In the 1980s most customers who drove Enterprise rentals were first-time renters. These customers were usually told about Enterprise by their insurance company and arrived at the Enterprise counter upset. They were not familiar with Enterprise and showed natural suspicion about renting a car from an unknown company.

"I'm not paying for anything," was often the first phrase out of the new renter's mouth as he stared across the counter at the smiling Enterprise employee.

While insurance companies could be dealt with rationally by the Enterprise sales force, the customers felt vulnerable and had to be convinced. An insurance customer whose car had been damaged by someone else was usually not happy to be paying for a rental. From the beginning Enterprise managers had drilled the customer service mentality into new recruits. The smiles behind the counter defused many an angry temper, and the com-

mitment to customer service became the glue that bound the Enterprise team together at a time when most customers did not recognize the Enterprise name.

While national advertising offered the prospect of much greater name recognition for Enterprise, it also raised a concern related to corporate strategy. Up until the commencement of national advertising, Enterprise had basically gone about its work quietly. It built customer relationships one by one. It located in inconspicuous, less-expensive areas and spent its time trying to figure out the competitors rather than waving flags in their faces.

The wrapped car in the 1980s marketing campaign quickly became an Enterprise icon. It was developed to build interest in and enthusiasm for the Enterprise way of doing business. The brown wrapping paper with the bold logo on the side far exceeded the original marketing expectations. Customers everywhere came to recognize and remember the image. Here, Jack Taylor and Bill Claggett, who was the catalyst for the successful marketing plan, reflect on the Enterprise wrap some years later.

Large-scale advertising meant that Enterprise could no longer slip into a new city unannounced and expect to have a trial period in which to test the waters and build a base of business. But advertising also meant that upon entering a new city, there would be many more people aware of Enterprise, and those people were more likely to become customers. (The heightened awareness of Enterprise would also make it easier to hire employees locally.)

After the first year marketing research showed that awareness of the Enterprise name had grown dramatically. The decision was made by Jack, Andy and the advertising committee to continue national advertising. In the second year the Enterprise advertising committee wanted more punch in the television advertising, and they asked the outside agency to develop several alternatives with greater visual impact.

The agency returned to the advertising committee with proposals of different approaches. The discussion quickly focused on one of the ideas as the committee stared at the picture of a car wrapped in brown paper like a parcel post package and stamped "Special Delivery."

"What is it?" somebody asked. There followed a lengthy discussion about the necessity of presenting customer service as a product. "Smiling faces can belong to people doing anything, but this car is the Enterprise image packaged as a product rather than as a nebulous service," was the reply from Jack Avrett and Frank Ginsberg, the two advertising men who had guided Enterprise through the creative process of advertising.

"I don't get it," said Jack. "It looks odd to me, and I don't want us to stand for something strange that people don't understand. But go ahead and run it and do the research, and let's see what happens."

The research quickly showed that television viewers liked it. That 15-second commercial grabbed people's attention and cut through the clutter of television advertising. Enterprise became the wrapped car in the minds of many viewers. Even though potential customers did not immediately comprehend all of the ramifications of "special delivery," the wrapped car became an icon that represented the Enterprise name and way of doing business. The advertising ran nationally, and the wrapped car took on a life of its own — it dramatically and memorably conveyed Enterprise's unique dedication to customer service.

By 1990 Enterprise had shed any vestiges of its former image as a low-key, Midwestern car company. The network of locations was quickly blanketing all parts of the country, and the unified national image boosted the company into the big leagues. While the explosive growth had far exceeded Jack's early expectations, he was pleased with the expansion because it held true to his vision — treating customers and employees fairly was the foundation upon which all aspects of the business were based. Just as Jack wanted, the growth continued to provide employees with greater opportunities. Andy's role

Once the impact of the wrapped car became clear, the advertising plan was expanded. Variations of the theme were used in many different forms of advertising, picking up on the high degree of name recognition potential customers demonstrated. Everything from cup coolers to print advertising carried the popular theme.

had grown considerably as he crafted the expansion plans and built the structure to sustain Jack's vision. It was now clear that both the vision and the structure were working and were sustaining the company's fast growth. There was no turning back, but more importantly, there was no reason to turn back: all the signals were "Go."

Used car sales have been part of the Enterprise business for many years. As Enterprise grew and the fleet of rental and leased cars expanded dramatically, car sales became an increasingly important part of Enterprise. The philosophy today in selling cars is the same philosophy Jack Taylor used as the foundation for used car sales years earlier — fixed prices for the cars accompanied by heavy doses of customer service. Opposite: Customer service, in fact, remains the focus of all Enterprise businesses, from rental to leasing to car sales.

$\mathscr{U}$PDATING THE BASICS

147

The dramatic expansion of the daily rental business across the country made clear that Enterprise's focus on a specific customer niche — the local customer — and its heavy emphasis on customer service were the critical ingredients for Enterprise's success. That niche was efficient (because adjusters influenced large numbers of customers) and profitable (because of high volume and repeat business). High-quality customer service had been the lifeblood of Jack's business since he first started leasing cars for Arthur Lindburg. As the rental formula for success became clearer, Jack and Andy began examining other parts of the Enterprise business to assess their market focus and customer service.

"You find me a top-quality Rolls Royce Silver Cloud a few years old, and I'll lease it from you," the doctor told Rick Snyder, standing in the Kingshighway office.

"Yes sir," responded Snyder. "I'll call you as soon as I can find one."

In the late 1970s Snyder was a 28-year-old leasing salesman in the Executive Leasing office on South Kingshighway, working with a diverse array of customers. There were upscale individuals like the doctor who wanted the Rolls Royce, middle-class working people who wanted economical, reliable transportation, and there were small businesses that needed small fleets for their salespeople. Snyder was eager to please his customers, but he was about to learn that it is not possible to be all things to all people, or to

148

please all the people all the time.

Snyder scoured the used car market in St. Louis looking for the right Rolls Royce for the doctor. He was ecstatic when he found it. It cost $25,000, but his math convinced him Executive would make money on the deal. He called the doctor, who came and looked at the car and told him it was fine. So Snyder bought the Rolls.

"Now put a sunroof in it," the doctor said. "Let me know when it's ready."

Snyder sighed, but having been well trained that taking care of the customer is the key to success, he took the Rolls to the shop for a sunroof. The mechanic took down the headliner and told Snyder it wasn't possible to put

a sunroof in the car. The car had an aluminum top and the rails to support the sunroof could not be properly secured to the roof of the Rolls.

Snyder called the doctor again, this time telling him in a very straightforward way that they could not put a sunroof in the Rolls.

"I don't want the car if you can't put a sunroof in it," was his terse reply.

Snyder never saw the doctor again, and now he was stranded with a $25,000 Rolls Royce. He shopped

The Enterprise leasing business was born in the basement of a Cadillac dealership and for many years attracted affluent customers. Leasing managers taught their people how to treat upscale customers and handle them with care. As the leasing business matured, it became increasingly apparent that the carriage-trade style of business was no longer the core of automobile leasing — anybody might be a good leasing prospect. Customers ranged from individuals with a simpler lifestyle to businesses needing entire fleets, not to mention the upscale customers from the early days looking for a gleaming Rolls Royce.

it all over town for a buyer, all to no avail. Finally he returned to the wholesaler who had sold him the car originally. That man said he would buy the car back, but for $20,000.

Snyder was dumbfounded. How could the deal have fallen apart so badly, and why was the car now worth so much less than a week earlier? He thought he was doing the right thing to please the customer, and he thought he had limited the risk by having the customer look at the car before he bought it. Now he was staring at a $5,000 loss. Because of the amount of the expected loss, Snyder talked with Andy. "What do you think I should do? Should I keep looking for a buyer closer to $25,000?" he asked.

"Sell it now, take the loss and be done with it. And don't forget it; it's an important lesson."

From its inception Executive Leasing had put a strong emphasis on satisfying customers, and that emphasis had served the company well. Business had grown steadily and losses were rare. Salesmen (they were all men in the early days) learned by emulating their bosses, and the selling process was intuitive. Good salesmen learned to sniff out a deal, and they learned how to close the deal. Executive Leasing sought to be "Everyman Leasing Company" in writing leases for all types of customers, both individuals and fleets for businesses.

But just as the energy crisis had been an unexpected external factor with a huge influence on the company in the 1970s, the over-capacity of the car manufacturers had an unexpected influence in the 1980s. By the late 1980s manufacturers had substantial excess production capacity and were eager to move cars any way they could. Rental companies benefited, as they were the recipients of favorable deals from the factories, but existing leasing companies found new and unexpected competition.

Manufacturers moved quickly and aggressively into the business of leasing cars to individuals. They formed captive leasing companies that, from the outset, were more competitive than any other companies in the market. They posted cheap lease rates and delivered vast numbers of cars very quickly through their network of dealers. Once a year manufacturers competed mercilessly with each other to be able to tout

"The number one selling car in America." In order to achieve the top volume, they had to strike deals that warmed the hearts of consumers but caused competitors to scratch their heads in dismay. When large numbers of cars came off lease and were returned to the manufacturers, they tackled the problem of oversupply by shipping the used cars overseas. (That tactic was not tried during the energy crisis because there was no market anywhere for gas guzzlers when gas was expensive.)

Enterprise Leasing tried, like others, to compete with the manufacturers. Though the basic leasing price to Enterprise's customers was often substantially higher than the lease price from the manufacturer, the manufacturer's lease generally had various restrictive covenants (such as termination penalties) that made the price differential difficult for the customer to understand. In light of these differences in both price and terms of leases, all Enterprise could do was focus on building customer loyalty by trying to provide more service than manufacturers. Maintenance and insurance plans were the most frequent ways Enterprise boosted the value of its leases, but with only limited overall

success. Enterprise steadily lost market share of the individual leasing business, a business that had been strong for the company since its earliest days as Executive Leasing.

By 1991 it was clear that there had been a structural change in the market and that things would never be the same again. Manufacturers had taken over the individual leasing business with their discounted rates, and the likelihood of anyone having a successful competitive edge in that market was dim. At the same time, large leasing companies such as Enterprise had committed substantial resources to develop fleets for big businesses that needed hundreds of vehicles — vehicles that had to be financed and maintained. Even though the geographic expansion of Enterprise had put more leasing salespeople in the field, the leasing business was not growing at an acceptable rate.

Rick Snyder had learned the hard way that trying to be all things to all people was fraught with trouble. While it was fun to deal with all types of cars (from the Taurus to the Rolls) and all types of customers (from the rich doctor to the small business), it was very hard to keep generating business without a more specific market focus.

Snyder was in charge of leasing at Enterprise in 1992, and he said that it was time to focus on a specific niche. Jack and Andy agreed. The world of leasing had changed, and Enterprise had to change with it.

The first step was to conduct market research. An outside consultant named Sandy Rogers was hired to help generate an unbiased view about which parts of the leasing market were the most attractive. He analyzed the market in terms of leasing customers and leasing competitors in order to find a niche where Enterprise could make money and grow.

"The Blueprint" (as the study was known) evolved very fast. Over the course of a few months, the research was completed and the decisions were made. Going forward the focus would no longer be "Everyman." Now the focus would be small, commercial fleets for businesses that needed 10 to 100 cars.

Real-world experience had made it clear that the individual market was no longer attractive because people were leasing directly from new car dealerships. (A few cities continued to generate profitable individual leases at Enterprise as a result of historical patterns of strong customer loyalty,

Throughout the 1980s, as national expansion roared forward at Enterprise, there was a careful effort to pay close attention to the automobile market. Enterprise managers from St. Louis corporate headquarters and rental and leasing offices across the country kept their eyes and ears open to learn new ways of responding to the rapidly changing world of cars and trucks. Fleet leasing for small- and medium-sized businesses was a market with many potential customers and an opportunity to put the Enterprise customer service philosophy to work in a new niche.

The legend of the lemon and the peach

(as told by the used car department of Executive Leasing.)

nce upon a time, there was a fast-talking lemon salesman who sold an innocent customer a used lemon. Within a very few weeks, the lemon went sour and so did the innocent customer. In another part of town, another innocent customer bought a real peach from Executive Leasing. Although the customer was a little fuzzy about automobiles . . . he drove away from Executive satisfied. You see, the Executive man knew all about the peach . . . even had a record of its pit stops. Don't ever buy a lemon . . . come by Executive and we'll find a peach of a used car for you.

EXECUTIVE LEASING

but those cities were no longer the predominant pattern.) The research showed that the major fleets, those of several hundred cars or more, were only growing at an annual rate of about 5 percent, a growth rate far below the 30 percent average annual growth for Enterprise's total business. It was the fleets serving smaller businesses across the country that were growing at a much faster rate.

Building on the market research, Enterprise refined the definition of its commercial leasing business. While customer service had always been an important factor, in the future, Enterprise would put even more emphasis on the overall service provided to the customer. By focusing on a customer segment that needed significant administrative services, Enterprise was able to offer a value-added product. They would not just sell a lease, but instead would sell the benefits of a fleet service company.

In conjunction with its emphasis on service, Enterprise was also able to emphasize its local presence. Leasing offices operating in 24 cities in 1997 could now provide close attention to

Throughout the 1980s and 1990s the used-car business continued to grow as the Enterprise fleet kept generating more and more rental and leased cars for resale. In the beginning it was a small part of the overall business. As car sales expanded, however, sales locations popped up all over the country, and car sales became another significant business opportunity.

152

With more used cars to sell, Enterprise increasingly focused on finding unique ways to sell cars. The traditional Enterprise fixed-price philosophy remained the same, but the marketing became more creative in reaching out to customers. Special sales events like these took place at off-site locations that could hold large numbers of cars and could create an extravaganza in order to sell cars quickly as the Enterprise pipeline of used cars continued to grow.

small businesses who wanted and needed support for their fleets. The larger competitors of Enterprise who tried to manage small fleets suffered from having to manage long-distance. The small, local companies did not have the clout of being able to deliver the full array of services that Enterprise could offer, some of which require large commitments of people and technology. (Maintenance and insurance programs call for complex systems and highly trained people, resources available to Enterprise, but not affordable for every leasing company.)

Finally, having redefined its niche in leasing, the question for Enterprise became one of staffing — how to recruit and motivate people. Two decades earlier, when leasing was the predominant business and rental was the unknown upstart, Enterprise excelled by emphasizing the growth potential in the leasing business. Occasionally rental managers were recruited from the leasing side of the business; usually it was the other way around.

Today it is the growth potential of the small fleet business that attracts managers in the leasing business. With a focus on a specific market that is large — and in the view of Enterprise underserved — the growth is expected to continue. Additional offices in more cities across the country are planned

From the earliest days of doing business, Enterprise found ways to go to its customers rather than waiting for customers to show up at its door. Expanding the car sales business meant going to the places where the customers were, and managers found creative ways to reach those customers. This manager took his sign with him.

as the emphasis continues on the high level of Enterprise service delivered to the customer locally.

Though these customers do not want to drive a Rolls Royce, they want a Rolls Royce level of service, and that is what Enterprise provides.

CAR SALES GO NATIONAL

In the early days of Executive Leasing, when Ray Covington managed the resale of the leasing fleet, most of the cars were sold to wholesalers. Covington gradually developed direct

sales to the consumer, both as a way to accommodate existing leasing or rental customers who wanted to buy a car and as a way to avoid the captive prices of wholesalers. The car sales business grew steadily, and various used car lots sprouted up at Enterprise locations as the leasing and rental business grew.

By the mid-1980s it was clear that there were structural changes both within the company and within the industry that called for a reexamination of Enterprise's car sales strategy. The Enterprise fleet was growing by leaps and bounds, and car dealers had

become more important participants in the rental business. (Many dealers had Enterprise rental people working in their own buildings, renting cars to the dealer's customers who dropped their cars off to be serviced.)

Paul Taylor, Jack's brother who joined Enterprise in the early 1980s to help with used car activities, took on the task of shaping a plan for selling used cars across the country, and for doing it more systematically. The goal was to sell more cars, but not to disturb the important dealer relationships that Enterprise had nurtured from its earliest days. As a former new car dealer himself, Paul was ideally suited to find a reasonable middle ground.

The thrust of the car sales strategy quickly evolved toward finding niches in the used car market that would not create direct competition with dealers. The niches that began to work best were those that involved referrals from other sources. Johnny Montgomery, a longtime member of the Enterprise team, persuaded credit unions and banks that Enterprise offered reliable used cars at reasonable prices and their members or customers could count on being treated fairly. Having several decades of experience selling cars for Enterprise and having weathered the energy crisis, Montgomery's skills were well suited for helping to carry out this new strategy.

During the late 1980s and early 1990s Enterprise sold used cars primarily through special event sales. Often these one- or two-day sales were for the members of a credit union or other referral group. These special event sales represented a toe in the water toward a more focused marketing of used cars.

The earliest special event sales were often unpredictable happenings. In Kansas City one sale was held in an enclosed arena. When the doors opened at 9:00 a.m., customers rushed in as if it were a bonanza not likely to be repeated. They climbed into cars and roamed through the arena, and when the sale ended, many, but not all, of the cars had been sold.

Therein lay much of the problem. It was difficult to anticipate the turnout for these sales; but more importantly, it was difficult to determine how many cars would be sold. While those cars that were sold generated a profit, the leftover cars often were sold at a loss. As a result, the financial impact was frequently mixed.

Over the years the car sales effort became much more refined. Direct mail was used to advertise the events, and systematic research could predict with reasonable accuracy how many people would attend. With accumulated experience under their belts, Enterprise managers also could anticipate how many cars would sell.

Gradually the emphasis shifted from special event sales to referral lots. These lots are locations that sell used cars every day, but most of their customers are Enterprise referrals. Today rental customers constitute a large percentage of used car buyers.

The thrust of the car sales business has been to create a profitable mechanism for selling some of the cars

With a more intensified effort to sell used cars, the Enterprise marketing effort became more creative and more systematic. Managers like Joe Diss in Washington, D.C., right, learned from each other how to make car buying fun. Huge off-site sales filled large arenas, below, but kept to the Enterprise practice of fixed prices and firm handshakes.

155

coming off lease and rental. The vast majority of the cars coming back to Enterprise are sold either to dealers or to wholesalers, with dealers getting the first shot at them. The national network of Enterprise car sales locations creates job opportunities for Enterprise employees, and it helps in the disposition of a fast-growing fleet.

Paul Taylor set out to formulate a plan for selling cars that would be sensitive to dealers and at the same time would create a way to sell used cars profitably. He avoided confrontation with dealers by focusing on customer segments not heavily emphasized by dealers. For the used car customers, his fixed-price system of selling used cars on referral lots treated them with the same respect Enterprise leasing and rental customers regularly received. He found a good niche in the market and applied heavy doses of customer service. The car sales strategy he developed was true to the Enterprise belief that if one treats others as one would like to be treated, profits will follow.

WHAT DO CUSTOMERS REALLY WANT?

In 1974, when Jack Taylor bought Keefe Coffee Company, his intent was to nurture a small entrepreneurial company to greater success. In addition to his own entrepreneurial interests in Keefe, Jack wanted to begin acquiring small, underdeveloped companies that could eventually generate career opportunities for employees and additional income for Enterprise. In 1975 the Enterprise Capital Group was established under the leadership of Doug Albrecht to manage these non-automotive businesses.

Soon Keefe was reasonably on track and generating increasing income. But Albrecht's work was not done. He had inherited the tangled issues of Mexican Inn and its products. At the end of two years, Albrecht and Andy agreed that it was time to get rid of Mexican Inn and move on to other opportunities.

Albrecht and Jack had lunch once a week at Busch's Grove to talk about non-automotive business prospects. Jack oversaw the constructive work that was being done to Keefe, and he agreed with it. At the same time, he communicated to Albrecht his feeling that any businesses they acquired should be based on the same philosophy as their core business — customer service would be the top priority.

An early acquisition was Coffee Butler Supply, a Keefe competitor based in South Carolina. Coffee Butler Supply counted among its customers six prisons in Florida for whom they provided instant coffee. Just as Albrecht was beginning to think about doing more business with prisons, he got a call from the Dade County Florida Correctional Institution. One of their senior administrators had stayed in a motel that had a Keefe instant coffeepot, and the prison was interested in individual coffeepots for their inmates.

Albrecht was intrigued by the fact that a car rental company might find a way to do worthwhile business with prisons. He began to explore the issue, trying to determine just what the correctional administrators really did need. After lengthy conversations with the prison managers at various levels, Albrecht found out that they didn't really want coffee in single service pouches like the motels, but they wanted coffee packaged in four-to-six-ounce packages for multiple servings.

Most of the competitive products were packaged in glass, and Albrecht knew that he had an advantage since the prisons' policies required them to re-package the coffee in safer plastic bags. Keefe began to package coffee in plastic pouches and also packaged powdered orange juice in plastic pouches. The people who ran the Florida prisons were eager to buy all the plastic pouches of instant coffee and orange juice they could get. (Inmates were allowed to mix the instant coffee with hot water on their own, and that was a popular step for the prison administrators to take.) Keefe's success with coffee and orange juice made it a regular supplier of consumable goods to correctional institutions.

Throughout the 1980s Albrecht built new packaging and marketing facilities for Keefe and continued to expand its product line. What had started as a simple coffeepot in small motels had grown into a large and thriving business. Keefe expanded its size and its product range and became a supplier to correctional institutions across the country for the full array of consumable products that line the shelves of prison commissaries. (Many of these commissaries now have the look of a quick-stop mini mart, with a repackaged line of products similar to those that people outside prison walls pick up every day.)

Each week as Albrecht and Jack reviewed their game plan, it was clear that the growth kept coming because Albrecht and his people kept listening to their customers. Granted, these customers were not car rental customers, but the underlying way of doing business was the same. Listening made it possible to fill a need that was not evident when the first call came for instant coffee for a Florida prison.

Other companies were acquired as the Capital Group grew. Some of them succeeded like the coffee and correctional businesses. Others did not work. After Mexican Inn, no acquisitions were so large or complex as to require substantial capital or management resources. The approach to acquisitions was refined so that they could become a management laboratory for fine-tuning the Enterprise business philosophy of learning new and different ways to listen to customers and to provide top-quality customer service.

By the mid-1990s the Enterprise Capital Group employed over 500 people, many of them employees who moved from car rental operations into the Capital Group companies. Jack's early desire to create a place where people could have expanded opportunities for career growth worked. Andy was the first to taste that opportunity at Keefe Coffee, and many others have followed that path.

Throughout the 1990s the Enterprise Capital Group expanded its business into a little-known market, correctional institutions. Over the years Keefe broadened its line of private label and convenience food items, and Crawford Supply, another member of the Enterprise Capital Group, developed diverse product lines (including personal care items, writing supplies and apparel) for federal, state and local corrections institutions across the country.

157

*E*xpansive skylines were becoming increasingly familiar scenes as Enterprise expanded rental, leasing and car sales throughout the 1980s. By the early 1990s new horizons were increasingly attractive, and the lure of new business continued to pull the company in new directions. Hawaii was the first foray into an unfamiliar culture. Opposite: With its aloha shirts and macadamia nuts, it seemed quite a bold change from the markets of the local Midwestern car company in earlier years.

Chapter Thirteen

ℰNTERPRISE CROSSES BOUNDARIES

"If it's good enough for the Bank of Hawaii, it's good enough for me. Order me a large."

Jack looked at the people around the table, and it was clear that the issue had been resolved. It was 1994, and for the first time in the course of Enterprise's expansion, a conflict between local practice and the Enterprise culture had been resolved in favor of local practice. For decades the business strategy had been tailored to fit the local market, but never had they tinkered with the Enterprise way of doing things. White dress shirts and ties and dresses were as much a part of their business as rental contracts.

For Enterprise the dress code is deeply linked with the company's history and culture. In the 1950s Jack had learned that one of the best ways to differentiate himself and his people from the competition was to look different.

"If we look different, we'll act different. I want these people to look like bankers when the customers walk in." Jack was emphatic from the earliest days — and he reminded anyone who deviated from the proper style of dress — that appearance does matter. Many an Enterprise employee over the years had questioned the necessity for ties after suffering the indignity of having one sucked up the vacuum hose while cleaning a car for a customer, but the ties remained.

159

When Enterprise first opened in Hawaii in 1994, the shirt-and-tie issue became an immediate concern. The team was successful in getting the office up and running, but they were fighting an uphill battle dealing with the local customs. Enterprise had long prided itself on being a company offering strong local autonomy, but Hawaiian print shirts (known as aloha shirts) were another matter.

Greg Stubblefield, a corporate manager from St. Louis, flew to Hawaii to assess the situation. He became self-conscious even before he arrived when he realized that he was the only person on the flight wearing a suit. After a lengthy visit in the local Enterprise office and after visiting several

banks just to see what the bank employees were wearing (the bank officers were all wearing aloha shirts), the Enterprise group went out to dinner to talk about what to do.

At the restaurant patrons from a nearby table wandered by the Enterprise crowd. They wanted to look more closely at this well-scrubbed, conservatively dressed group of people who were sitting up straight in their chairs. One of the patrons looked at the men's white shirts and ties and asked, "Are you missionaries?"

Stubblefield offered a weak smile, shook his head and replied in a low voice, "No, we're not missionaries. We're in the car rental business."

"Ohhhhh," the confused Hawaiian responded, and as he walked back to his own table, there seemed to be unresolved doubt as to whether these people in neckties were in fact missionaries. Or were they perhaps white-collar crooks? After dinner it was clear that the strong recommendation to Jack and Andy would be to approve aloha shirts for Enterprise people in Hawaii.

Once Jack knew that the bankers weren't wearing coats and ties, he was

Wayne Tanaka, pictured on the right with the Aiea staff, worked hard planting the Enterprise culture in new soil. They used the well-established customer service formula and found it was as effective in Hawaii as it had been for many years on the mainland. Fine-tuning was always a challenge, but their enthusiasm brought about rapid growth in this new market.

satisfied with the aloha shirts, as long as the Enterprise people dressed like the bankers. Thus the Enterprise culture became adaptable without compromising its foundations. Jack's early commitment to the coat-and-tie dress code was intended to give the most favorable impression to the customer and to make Enterprise employees feel proud of the way they presented themselves. If they could best do that in aloha shirts, it was all right with him. (The Enterprise aloha shirts have button-down collars, so that provides one bit of continuity in the dress code.)

As the international expansion began to move from the drawing boards to the streets, Enterprise managers would frequently be confronted with issues of cultural differences — style of dress, language and ways of interacting with customers would all pose challenges. The fine line to be navigated would mean adhering to the core values of how Enterprise employees present themselves and treat customers, yet being sensitive to the differences in cultures.

CROSSING NEW FRONTIERS

Expansion outside the United States grew out of a pragmatic concern in the

Jack Taylor had always been a real stickler about how his employees dressed. "I want you to look like bankers," he said repeatedly, and so they did. It took some persuading to convince him that in Hawaii even the bankers wore aloha shirts, opposite below, but once he was convinced, the Enterprise managers took to aloha shirts like fish to water. The coaster, opposite above, is a memento from the restaurant where the Enterprise managers first confronted the stigma of "missionary" dress from local Hawaiians.

late 1980s that sooner or later there would be no new major markets for Enterprise within the United States. Continuing expansion had been so embedded within the Enterprise culture that managers throughout the organization had come to expect that there would always be significant opportunities on the horizon. The managers had learned to make short-term sacrifices (both reduced pay and more hard work) in order to be able to grab a brass ring in the future.

These anticipated opportunities were very real, as people did continue to move ahead while national expansion efforts rolled forward. If the growth should slow down significantly, these aggressive managers would have to wait until someone ahead of them quit, got

fired or died (all fairly rare occurrences in a healthy young company). Absent a belief in future opportunities, there was a large risk that Enterprise would lose its single most critical resource — highly motivated and enthusiastic managers. And the company was not about to let that happen.

Once international expansion was mapped out as the company's next strategic move, the plan for carrying out that strategy was patterned after Enterprise's early expansion in the United States. In the 1960s national expansion focused on moving into more familiar areas before tackling tougher ones. Thus Enterprise's first step into the international arena was to think about how Canada might fit as a logical progression of Enterprise's strategy for

161

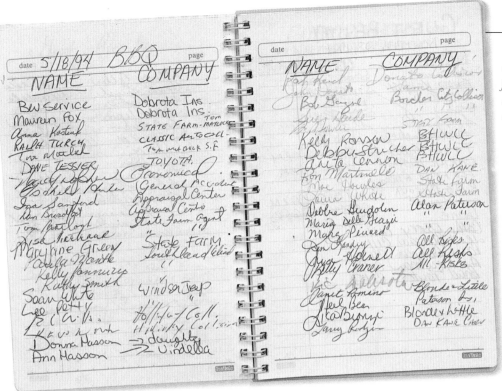

The notebook, left, was a "guest book" from an open house that Jacques Juneau had in the early days of the Windsor office. Such activities helped Enterprise make ties with local businesses in the community that would later provide referrals. Enterprise's first expansion outside the U.S. has been very successful, and now most of Canada is served by Enterprise.

growth into new markets.

A few Enterprise managers started reading the daily newspapers from Toronto and Vancouver in order to learn about how life in Canada compared to life in the U.S. The sports pages showed the greatest common ties, and the news about Canadian politics was the most foreign element to the Midwesterners. As they became more aggressive in doing their homework, they began to shape the bare bones of an expansion strategy. The strategy was to get into the market in a relatively comfortable location and learn as much as possible about the ways of doing business in Canada before opening in new locations.

The business plan focused on building relationships with insurance companies and body shops to generate replacement rental business, becoming part of the local business community and generating word-of-mouth referrals by providing uncompromising service to customers. (Even with increased advertising, the Enterprise strategy continued to focus on repeat business and personal referrals as the best way to get business. The advertising created name recognition and awareness of the Enterprise image, but most of the time it was still personal ties that brought business into the rental office.)

On February 3, 1993, a Texan named Jacques Juneau crossed the Detroit River to Windsor, Ontario, and opened the first Enterprise office in Canada. Windsor was a medium-sized Canadian city separated from Detroit only by the Detroit River. The new office could call on Enterprise managers in Detroit for help when needed. Juneau's job was to start the Canadian presence in a small city where the competition was not so fierce.

As was often the case in the U.S., the office was not ready for the new Enterprise occupants. Juneau met the landlord and picked up the key, then discovered that expected renovations had not been done. The contractors had only finished putting the studs in place, and the office space was not yet usable. After a week of cajoling and arm twisting, the space was finished, and the furniture, forms and equipment were in place.

Despite the fact that the office itself was unfinished, Juneau set out immediately to get his fleet in place and to start building business ties. He purchased 25 cars from a local dealer his first day in Windsor. Two days later, still before the office was habitable, he rented a car to his first customer, a referral from the dealer who sold him the cars for his fleet. By the end of his first month in Canada Juneau had 12 cars on rent, and he had hired two Canadians to work as part of the Enterprise team. Juneau had crossed a frontier for Enterprise. Within three months the Windsor team had 100 cars on rent. The flag was being carried forward as he and his fledgling team began the process of selling themselves, their services and their company in a new part of the world.

Enterprise had to make a few adjustments in its usual way of doing business. When they visited a local body shop to introduce themselves and get to know the employees there, they were greeted with confusion rather than welcome. The body shop foreman did not understand why they were there, and he felt obliged to pay for the doughnuts Juneau had brought as a gift. Once Juneau sat down and explained that the doughnuts were brought along to break the ice and make it easier to talk with them as a prospective customer (a typical practice in the U.S.), the foreman accepted the doughnuts, the conversation started and the foundations of a crucial business relationship were laid.

The competitors in Canada did not acquiesce quietly to the arrival of Enterprise. Insurance adjusters reported to Juneau that competitors were calling on them with a vigor the adjusters had not seen in years. It was the Enterprise service as well as the attractive rates that had caught the eye of the adjusters, and the competitors were quick to act.

While Enterprise was moving rapidly into Canada, a competitor who was already operating in Canada quickly attempted to register the Enterprise name for its own use to thwart Enterprise's expansion efforts. For the first time, Enterprise saw a vulnerability in its image with the recognition that it might not be able to use its own name in Canada. The earlier experience with the name shift from Executive Leasing to Enterprise Leasing, and then from Enterprise Leasing to Enterprise Rent-A-Car,

had made it clear that a unified corporate image was important in a time of rapid expansion.

Litigation commenced in Canada when Enterprise went to court to obtain full rights to the use of its name in Canada. While the court arguments were being led by the lawyers, the Enterprise managers were operating under the name "Ecars" in order to avoid heightening the conflict. As the Enterprise locations known as Ecars grew in number throughout Canada, the front-line sales people were, for the

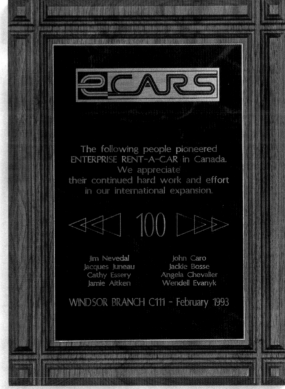

The medallion below commemorated the opening of the 100th Enterprise office in Canada. The plaque at right identifies the original members of the Windsor office, Enterprise's first office in Canada.

ECARS

The following people pioneered ENTERPRISE RENT-A-CAR in Canada. We appreciate their continued hard work and effort in our international expansion.

◁◁◁ 100 ▷▷▷

Jim Nevedal
Jacques Juneau
Cathy Essery
Jamie Aitken

John Caro
Jackie Bosse
Angela Chevalier
Wendell Evanyk

WINDSOR BRANCH C111 - February 1993

163

first time, competing against the name Enterprise, which their competitor had begun to use. Eventually Enterprise prevailed in court and gained the exclusive right to use its name in Canada.

Enterprise grew rapidly in Canada, and the managers worked hard to minimize its image as a big, U.S.-based company. Just as Don Ross had done 20 years earlier in Kansas City, the Canadian managers bought cars locally, banked locally, hired locally and participated fully in the life of the community, to demonstrate their local commitment. They drew on Enterprise's knowledge and resources, but theirs was a local presence in the towns and cities of Canada. They immersed themselves in the civic affairs of the towns where they lived and worked.

As a company immersed in the local Canadian markets, Enterprise saw itself as a David, not a Goliath, of the Canadian rental industry. Enterprise employees raised the standard of the level of service insurance companies could expect to receive for replacement rentals, and they did it in the tried-and-true Enterprise way of calling on insurance companies and body shops one by one. By approaching these new

markets in the way a younger and more vulnerable local company would operate, they would then become the spoiler when they stepped on the toes of their giant Canadian competitors. And step on competitor toes they did, as they established in Canada the higher standard of customer service that had become synonymous with the Enterprise way of doing business.

Between 1993 and 1996 the Enterprise presence in Canada grew from one fledgling office in Windsor to a national network of 175 offices from one end of Canada to the other.

ANOTHER FOREIGN FRONTIER: ENGLAND

They were lined up five and six deep, young people with eager faces crowded around the Enterprise booth at the London graduate recruitment fair in June 1994. The fairs were a new experience for the three Enterprise managers from the U.S. who were there to recruit new employees for the first Enterprise office in England.

"But where are you located?" one confused young man kept asking over the din of the crowd.

"All over the U.S., and we'll be

In the United Kingdom the more things changed, the more they stayed the same. Customer service was the same — going the extra mile to take care of the customer — but the insurance business operated differently there than it did in the United States. Enterprise managers adapted to the different environment, and the business grew rapidly. Early on they learned to put the "e" logo on the other side of the car so it would be behind the driver, just as it is in the United States.

164

here shortly," was the reply.

"But I don't follow your reasoning," the young man persisted. "Are you saying that you're intent upon hiring people to work here before you've actually set up an office in the U.K.?"

That was exactly the point. "We're starting with recruiting because people are the critical factor in making our business succeed," the Enterprise managers responded repeatedly as the question arose time and time again. But the Enterprise managers were selling something they had never sold before — dreams. Throughout the United States for nearly 30 years there had been a growing network of offices to point to as the backbone of the company. While local hiring was a critical part of the Enterprise way of doing business, not since the early Executive Leasing days had it required such a leap of faith for a new recruit to see the substance and the potential of the company.

The year 1994 was a grim year in England in terms of job prospects for graduates recently out of school. The recession that had racked the country had just subsided, and good jobs were still scarce. Companies were growing

The face of Enterprise in the United Kingdom was the same familiar face seen across America. Offices sprouted up quickly, like the Wigan office in Manchester, left, and the Birmingham office, below. Inside the offices was an increasingly diverse blend of people, some transferred from Enterprise offices in the United States and Canada and some hired from towns near Enterprise locations in the U.K.

cautiously, and no one had ever heard of a company hiring people months before the opening of its first office.

As thousands of his peers milled about trying to find some advantage over each other in the search for elusive, promising jobs, Adam Hitchmough worked his way to the front of the crowd at the Enterprise booth. Unlike many of his peers, Hitchmough had already worked and traveled for two years after having finished school. He honed in on the Enterprise booth because he felt instinctively that there were substantive rewards associated with what certainly appeared to be a significant risk with an unproved foreign company.

"My friends thought I was absolutely crazy," Hitchmough recalled

later. "Maybe so, but I was running on blind faith that I could trust these people." Enterprise had found that it could sell its dream on the other side of the Atlantic Ocean.

The "crazy" risk paid off for Hitchmough, and he was offered a job, still some months before the opening of the first office in the U.K. He became part of the team that opened the Enterprise office in Reading, England, in September 1994 under the leadership of Paul Bolda. Bolda was a well-experienced Enterprise manager who had been in the forefront of the expansion into Canada. Now his mettle was to be tested more severely in the U.K.

In the tradition of Enterprise expansion elsewhere, the first foothold was in a place removed from the competitive uncertainties of the biggest cities. Reading is just over 30 miles west of London, and it is a hub of commerce that is not unlike St. Louis. Its economic growth was clearly evidenced by the high-tech companies that made Reading their home, and the business climate felt comfortable to the first Enterprise managers who visited there.

Enterprise learned in Canada that a local approach to marketing could be successful even in the absence of an extensive national network of offices. Because in England the insurance replacement business was handled by the body shops rather than by the insurance companies, aggressive and persistent sales calls to the body shops became the focus of the Enterprise effort. Hitchmough and the other Enterprise people in England found that the businesspeople in Reading were receptive to their sales pitch for car rentals.

The personal sales call approach that the local staff in Reading used was one that they learned from Paul Bolda

and the other highly experienced senior managers who had been sent to England to oversee the initial efforts. With only one office and a heavy concentration of seasoned Enterprise managers, local staff like Hitchmough and other Enterprise employees learned the business from very experienced mentors.

Just as Hitchmough had taken the job at Enterprise on faith, he converted customers to the Enterprise fold by persuading them to put their trust in him and in the services he could provide. The Enterprise name was unknown to his prospects, so the critical task was convincing customers to believe in him personally and in his ability to deliver the Enterprise capabilities.

The local efforts were increasingly successful, and one month after the Reading office opened, an office was opened in Slough. It, too, kept a local focus to its sales and marketing and, like the team in Reading, found a growing interest in doing business with this upstart American company that was building business rapidly. As the body shops began to do business with Enterprise, personal referrals had a ballooning effect on the businesses' growth. The word-of-mouth advertising in St. Louis that had been crucial in

Enterprise's early history was being repeated now on foreign shores.

Hitchmough's blind faith was gradually being translated into a track record of success. But the success was not without doubts. "I hit the wall at the six-month mark. I just didn't know if it would work. But then I realized this was the make or break point; there was no choice but to make it work. So we did."

By the spring of 1995 several more offices were opened. For the first time Enterprise could begin to see the outline of a national presence in England. With a national presence would come the ability to market to the large national insurance companies on a direct basis. By 1996 the number of Enterprise offices in England passed 50, and the national marketing effort commenced.

Convincing British insurance companies that there was a better way of providing replacement vehicle service did not happen overnight. But with a national network of offices in place and with a growing number of satisfied body shops as customers, the Enterprise way of doing business began to look more promising in England.

While the Enterprise goal was to generate business rather than to come

Current locations as of January '97

in as reformers of the existing system, they were willing to be reformers if that was what was needed. They began building business in England just as they had done it elsewhere. They grew customer by customer as they worked through the existing system of working with body shops and seeking their referrals.

But as their national network grew, the Enterprise managers began aggressively marketing their services to insurance companies, eager to convince them to deal directly with Enterprise. By 1996 Enterprise was emerging in England as a national force that could deliver highly efficient replacement service to insurance companies. Enterprise was now able to offer U.K. insurance companies the full array of administrative and customer service advantages it had made available to U.S. insurance companies for many

years. The marketing pitch to the U.K. insurers was that Enterprise could make their lives easier and simpler by offering one-stop shopping for replacement rentals.

The Enterprise foundation in the U.K. was solid — it had been constructed in the traditional Enterprise way of building business only at the pace at which it could fully deliver its promises.

As the Enterprise business grew rapidly in the United Kingdom, there was reason to celebrate. The pride of accomplishment was more important than the fancy dress. By 1997 Enterprise had 100 offices in the United Kingdom, an extraordinary rate of growth in a new market. The formula for expansion had been taken to new heights as the company both held to the tried and true philosophy and made critical adjustments so they could thrive in a different market. And thrive they did.

167

By 1996 the annual meeting of Enterprise rental managers had grown to a group of over 3,000 people. A far cry from the annual gathering in the Pine Room at Busch's Grove in St. Louis, this meeting required the Coliseum in San Antonio and several hotels. Though the size and location changed significantly, the purpose of the managers' meeting remained the same — stay in touch with the core philosophy, share ideas with colleagues and have fun. Opposite: The "EQ Test" became a popular marketing and recruiting tool in the mid-1990s.

$\mathcal{T}$HE ENTERPRISE TEAM

As if to draw a line in the sand in front of the competition, the annual meeting of Enterprise rental managers in 1996 was held in San Antonio, Texas, across the street from the Alamo. It was a hot, clear day when managers, first by the hundreds then by the thousands, began checking into a handful of downtown San Antonio hotels. It was like a college reunion, people laughing and hugging when they came across friends they had not seen since the meeting last year. They were greeted at the hotels by a support team of Enterprise people in red polo shirts and khaki shorts armed with cellular phones and laptop computers ready to register them for this once-a-year event.

Upon arrival, each manager was given a packet of materials. The participants held out their arms and had plastic hospital-style bracelets snapped on over their wrists. The wrist bands were the subject of some laughter, but they stopped questioning the bands when asked "Would you rather have a chain around your neck with a dog tag? This not only gets you in the meetings but also gets you free beers at the end of the day." By the time they were all there, the front-line managerial troops of over 3,000 people were in place for information, inspiration and fun.

Jack Taylor has always put trust in younger people. He feels that if the company hires the right ones and trains them well, there will be a long-term supply of strong managerial talent. It has also been his thinking that customers will be more forgiving of well-meaning, but imperfect, people when they make mistakes if they are honest about their mistakes and try to straighten out customers' problems.

Since the earliest days of Executive Leasing, Jack has hired people right out of school so he could train them to work in a way that is consistent with his style. He has instilled in these people his own values about how to work with other people, both customers and

Though the Enterprise team values friendly interpersonal relationships, hard-driving intellect and technology are a critical underpinning for growth and success. Marc Cohn shepherded the company into a new world of high-tech customer service. He built a computer network that opened the door to new expansion opportunities while Andy Taylor stood at the helm and guided the direction of the company's growth.

fellow employees. At the same time, he has encouraged independent thinking about new or different ways of doing things, and over the years his work force has become increasingly diverse.

Jack Taylor has built a team of people who share a common foundation in the business principle he lives by — treat others as you would like to be treated. But these people are far from being wind-up clones of Jack Taylor. The company is populated with independent thinkers who can disagree with each other in the process of sharing ideas, but they all are grounded in the same basic values. What they do might

vary from one person to another, but how they do it reflects a common belief of treating others fairly.

Enterprise employees are pragmatic problem solvers. In their work they act like participants in a giant game of intramurals in which players form teams and compete hotly with their friends from down the hall or across the quadrangle. And yet these hotly competitive friends are part of a larger team, one that is ultimately far more important than the daily lineup in their own branch. How the whole company performs supersedes the performance of any one branch, and they all know that.

For most employees, their job at Enterprise is their first full-time job. Rarely are people hired from other companies. (Those that are hired from elsewhere, like Marc Cohn from IBM, come to Enterprise to perform jobs that require a specialized background.) The Enterprise team only knows the Enterprise way, and only a few have had exposure to the cultures of other corporations. They have never experienced a layoff (Enterprise has never had a "downsizing"), and their loyalty to the culture of fair treatment is the bond that keeps the team working as a tightly constructed unit. The up-and-coming managers of Enterprise have become the transmitters of the corporate culture. As they have received fair treatment from their managers, they treat customers and colleagues fairly. From each wave of new recruits comes a core of dedicated team players who carve out a bright future for themselves at Enterprise. This team both transmits and defines the culture for those around them.

The army of friendly faces that filled the convention hall in San Antonio looked like it could take on any challenge. The men and women were clean-cut, well-dressed professionals, as comfortable in a meeting as

Women Can Give Rides to
MEN THEY DON'T KNOW

In 1974 Jack's daughter, Jo Ann, was a recent college graduate and wanted to work in the rental business at Enterprise. Jack was flattered that she wanted to work in the family business, but he was adamant that she could not work in the daily rental business.

"Young women do not wash cars and they do not pick up strange men," he told her. Jo Ann persisted. Jack agreed that she could work in a branch, but her job would be administrative, not a job at the rental counter. Though his attitude was one of concern and caution, it revealed an inherent challenge for young women eager to enter the rental business.

Jo Ann went to work in the Des Peres office in St. Louis. Bud Schleicher, a veteran manager who had learned the ropes under Jack's tutelage years earlier, was in charge of that office. Schleicher ran that office the way he had been taught to manage — everybody pitched in, even the boss's daughter. As a result, Jo Ann did work behind the rental counter fairly often when business was hectic, and she did pick up and deliver cars to men she did not know.

Twenty years later no one, not even Jack, thinks twice about two of Jack's granddaughters, Jo Ann's daughter Carolyn Kindle and Andy's daughter Chrissy Taylor, working behind the counter at Enterprise rental offices. During the 1980s Enterprise actively recruited many women, and their ability to be successful in the business had become clear.

Part of the change in hiring patterns was a reflection of the overall social change that had taken place in the business world during those years, and part of it resulted from the actions of pragmatic and forward-thinking managers who helped Enterprise respond to these changing times. Most importantly, however, the women at every level of Enterprise have worked to prove that they are just as assertive and capable as their male counterparts.

The Changing Face of
ENTERPRISE

In the early days Jack and his lieutenants did all of the hiring. Many employees, like customers, learned about Enterprise by word-of-mouth communication. The interview style was relaxed, but from the start the emphasis in recruiting was on finding people who were industrious and motivated, and who could relate well to other people.

Throughout the early expansion days, managers were responsible for the local recruiting activities. In the 1980s Bill Holekamp hired the first Enterprise recruiter in California because hiring

needs were growing too fast for the managers to handle effectively. That first recruiter was met with some internal concern and skepticism by many people who wanted to continue recruiting the old-fashioned way.

In 1996 Enterprise hired over 10,000 recent college graduates. There are recruiters in each Enterprise group solely

responsible for finding and hiring the right number of people to keep the pipeline full of new "eager beavers."

In conjunction with its stepped-up approach to large-scale recruiting on college campuses all across the country, Enterprise launched its first website on the Internet and developed the "EQ Test." Callaway Ludington was

the Enterprise manager who saw the potential and the importance of developing an "Enterprise Quotient" to assist in recruiting.

"EQ" also stands for "emotional quotient," and the simply structured brochure of questions makes clear that the success factors at Enterprise have more to do with "people" skills than with traditional measures of intellect found in IQ tests. Decades of experience have made clear that these interpersonal skills and leadership qualities are critical factors for success at Enterprise.

In the earliest days of the company, people were hired from St. Louis because that was where the business was. By the 1990s, with business expanding rapidly in distant locations, recruiting became a critical activity. Recruiters traveled to college campuses across America and attended recruiting sessions in Europe to find the right people for the local offices. The critical ingredient for success at Enterprise has always been the ability to deal effectively with other people. On the Internet and at campus events, thousands of college students take the few minutes to put themselves to the "EQ Test."

behind the wheel. All of them had an all-American look that comes from a high school yearbook rather than from a movie magazine. Their pictures would have shown up as "Best Personality" or "Most Athletic," and nearly all were class leaders in some way.

The first day, more senior area managers heard from corporate managers from St. Louis and participated in a variety of small-group sessions to probe ongoing issues. They were divided into groups, assigned to hotel conference rooms and arranged around rectangular tables facing each other. The group facilitator started the discussion, and the managers sat straight up, leaning forward attentively, with elbows resting on the table. They were courteous to each other and communicated directly with animated voices. It wasn't just an exchange of information, it was an exchange of ideas about what worked best in their own offices. They pushed each other to articulate not only what they were doing in particular areas, but why it was working. We have a callback center, too. How do you consolidate the calls in Boston? And what about the body shops, why do you handle them that way?

Customer service, competition, sales and marketing, staffing — the sessions moved back and forth between the big picture and the day-to-day concerns of front-line managers. How do we recruit enough high-quality people? How do we motivate the car preps (the people who wash and vacuum the cars)? How do you provide leadership by example when your tie has just been sucked up the vacuum hose?

The discussions were facilitated by senior managers from corporate headquarters who would prod and nudge but generally not instruct the group. When asked "What's corporate's view on that issue?" the usual reply was, "I'm not sure corporate's view on that issue is important; it is more important to understand what works in your area and why."

Every hour-and-a-half from 8:30 in the morning until 5:00 in the evening, the hotel lobbies were overwhelmed by a swarm of managers who moved from one session into another. They chatted enthusiastically with friends who had benefited from the large number of job promotions during the year. These were friends who had not seen each other since the prior year's rental meeting.

An Enterprise manager from upstate New York who was transferred to England described her experience to a colleague with whom she used to work:

"I think England today is a new frontier for Enterprise, like the U.S. was in the 1960s. It is a huge opportunity to build a new business from scratch, and I love it. It's great personally, too; you only live once. I'm meeting people from all over. In our branch we have Hindus and Sikhs as well as English people and Americans like me. We're working hard to build relationships with insurance companies and body shops, and I know we'll look back on it someday and be really glad we were there. You should come over, try it."

The exchange of ideas in the problem-solving sessions served to reinforce the corporate culture, and these exchanges about their personal experiences were more than the reuniting of old friends. Both the sessions and the catching up with friends spread the experiences of each individual within the company. Their collective experiences became a renewed definition of the company's culture.

Friday night was party time, a night off. All 3,000 climbed on buses at 6:30 and went to the coliseum for a rodeo organized and performed just for this group. Jeans, boots, bandannas and cowboy hats replaced the neatly pressed khakis of the workday sessions. Tubs of cold beers were ready at

173

the coliseum as thousands of rental managers filled the stands, and the show began.

The lights dimmed, and a woman on horseback rode to the center of the arena. The spotlight focused on her, and the American flag she carried began to ripple behind her as she rode around the ring. The crowd cheered.

Even on their night off, the managers continued to share each others' knowledge and empathy. They mingled through the stands and the halls, their constant talking getting louder in response to the competition from the hooting and hollering around them. They looked for friends, they talked fun and they talked business.

"I tell my 90-day employees, 'Look, you might do four out of five things right, but that's not enough. It may be okay for you, but what about when you're competing with people who do five out of five things right?' I have to keep working with them so they understand how the whole team functions. Then when they get it right, it is great to watch them do well."

A hush came over the crowd when the cowboys started the calf-roping competition. For the first time in several days, the entire crowd was subdued and, briefly, quiet. The cowboys threw their lassoes around the calves, jerked them back by their necks and threw them to the ground. There were a few boos, then like a wave, the boos rumbled through the coliseum. These people who themselves are extremely competitive have been taught relentlessly to treat others as you would like to be treated. Seeing animals being jerked backwards by their necks bothered them. Some turned away and talked with their neighbors. Others walked out to the hallway under the stands for another beer.

In contrast to the boos at the rodeo, there was endless enthusiasm the following night at the dinner in the hotel's grand ballroom. The room was a sea of fresh faces with wide smiles and white teeth. They were now in business dress, dark suits and white

From the Ozarks to San Antonio, Enterprise managers work hard and have fun. After a full day of meetings, seminars and mind-stretching activities, relaxation eases the brain and renews old friendships at Enterprise gatherings everywhere.

shirts for the men and simple suits and dresses for the women. This was not a party, it was business.

These Enterprise managers are a group with increasing diversity, yet they have common traits of the Enterprise culture. It is the stuff inside, the energy, motivation, attitude and vocality that define them as similar. Those traits define who these people are and how they present themselves. What you see is what you get; this is who they are.

Waiters and waitresses glided through the room, balancing trays of steak and potatoes, and gradually the room became warmer. As the attendees took off their suit jackets, the room was increasingly dotted with white shirts. The dinner conversation sounded like a

Channeling enthusiasm can be a challenge. Hard-charging managers get used to long hours behind the counter and countless sagas of customer service that would make many business school case studies seem no more useful than a sail on a windless sea. They discipline themselves to work hard, and that same energy bursts out whenever they gather in groups.

subdued buzz, a notch below the usual level of excitement.

After dinner the attention focused on the podium. Because the three-day meeting had been a success, the first order of business was to thank the support team who handled the logistics of the meeting and were critical to its success. That team was seated in the back of the room, and when they stood, the crowd instantly rose and gave an ovation to the people who did the gritty hard work of making the meeting happen.

The next speaker was Don Ross, who introduced himself as "the shortest guy with the longest title." Ross, the senior executive vice president and chief operating officer, told the crowd where Enterprise ranked in the world of car rentals.

"We have grown to 320,000 cars

in our rental fleet as of the end of fiscal year 1996. There is no doubt we are the largest car rental company in the United States."

The crowd treated him warmly as a beloved and respected leader who had been on the front lines in guiding the company's growth. His efforts to slow down their ovation when he finished were futile. They clapped long and hard. Then there was a pause after the crowd finally settled down, and Ross introduced "our founder and chairman, Jack C. Taylor."

The room roared. What might have been mistaken earlier for an energetic political rally now looked like part revival, part rally, part concert, part sports championship, and in every way an explosion of emotion not

commonly seen in business today. Every one of the thousands of managers shot up out of their seats as if they had waited all year for this moment. They clapped, but mostly they shouted. Their affection was like a surge of electricity.

Jack Taylor stood there facing his troops with his white hair gleaming and his own smile beaming large on the two giant video screens that hung on either side of the podium. He accepted their acclamation graciously and then began to talk.

"I should be congratulating and clapping for you rather than having you clap for me, because you are the reason for the success of this company. Maybe I had a fairly decent idea early on, but in no way could we have had the success we've had without the contribution

175

GIVING BACK
to the Community

In 1980 a strong sense of social responsibility led to the formation of the Enterprise Rent-A-Car Foundation in order to give benefits back to the communities that had made possible the company's phenomenal growth. From the outset, the objective of the Foundation has been to work on a very personal level. Its focus has been on reaching out to many parts of the Enterprise family by providing many small grants rather than only a few very large grants.

The Foundation was set up in a unique way to involve Enterprise employees. The Foundation distributes its resources in response to requests coming primarily from Enterprise employees, who in some cases are forwarding requests from cus-

tomers. There are no set categories into which grants are made. It is the nature of the requests that determines which causes will be supported. The efforts of the Foundation include the company's support for the United Way, which matches a portion of donations given by employees. Enterprise and its employees are known as very significant supporters of the United Way throughout the U.S. In addition to the United Way, the Foundation supports over 400 organizations.

In the early years of the Foundation, many of the contributions were to diverse organizations in St. Louis, ranging from women's self-help centers and child abuse centers to the Children's Hospital. In addition to his

The Enterprise Rent-A-Car Foundation has been an important and visible indicator of the company's commitment to its local communities and to the larger Enterprise family. Every year the company funds the Foundation with a portion of corporate profits, and a diverse board makes decisions about supporting particular needs. Jo Ann Taylor Kindle oversees the Foundation's board.

duties as vice president at Enterprise, Van Black was the first Foundation manager. Proposals for funding were submitted for review and approval to its board, which included Jack Taylor, Susan Taylor, Jo Ann Kindle and Marianne Knaup. In 1995

Van Black retired, and Jack's daughter, Jo Ann Kindle, now serves as president of the Foundation.

Today the structure of the board includes rotating senior Enterprise managers as well as members of the corporate staff in order to help encourage a broad outlook in giving to causes that have a direct impact on the lives of Enterprise people and the communities Enterprise is a part of.

Not only have Enterprise employees given tirelessly of their time, but they have contributed significant amounts of money to important local efforts. The bat below was a gift from the United Way of Greater St. Louis in 1996 to acknowledge a contribution from Enterprise and its individual employees in a record amount — over $1 million.

When Jack Taylor addressed the rental managers in San Antonio, the crowd roared an enthusiastic welcome for their much-beloved leader. Then they listened intently as the chairman thanked them for their work. The founder and the rental managers once again had an opportunity to reaffirm the Enterprise philosophy and carry it forward to a new, larger generation of team members.

that each and every one of you has made every day with your long hours, your hard work, your caring for the customer, your caring about the company and your caring about each other. It is truly gratifying for me to see not only how you radiate good feelings toward me, which I greatly appreciate, but also the good feelings and camaraderie amongst yourselves. Thank you from the bottom of my heart, you have made me a very happy 74-year-old guy.... Thank you very much."

Another ovation rocked through the room. These people who follow him share common beliefs and values, and they revere the man who made this business life possible for them.

Finally the crowd settled back, and Andy Taylor came to the podium, again surrounded by the roar that has become the trademark greeting to the people that matter in their business.

Andy started by saying, in his natural style of nonpartisanship, "the Democrats and Republicans have nothing on us when it comes to putting on a successful convention." He then added, "I can just tell you that Jack and I and my sister, Jo Ann, and the rest of our family are committed to all of you and to your success.

"First of all, I want to congratulate you on another record-breaking year." He then recounted the performance of the company's rental business over the past year. He made clear the high points and reminded the group of the areas that still need continuing attention. It was all business from the boss, and the room was hushed. He spelled out the numbers of promotions in the past year, and he described the opportunities for growth on the horizon.

"This is a great time to be part of a super company, your company. Think customer satisfaction, think employee motivation. If you get those things right, the bottom line

will certainly happen."

The lights went up, and the crowd started to file out the rear of the room. After a few minutes most of the thousands were gone, but a large crowd of people 10 to 15 deep continued to crowd around Andy and Jack Taylor in the front of the room, shaking hands and taking pictures.

For these managers, the time together in San Antonio was more than corporate bonding. They were inspired by Jack and they were congratulated by Andy as they looked back at the past year's work. Both their hearts and their minds had been renewed as they left the meeting.

Like sailors on a brief shore leave, the crowd headed for the watering holes of San Antonio to swap war stories. On Monday they would be back on board the "ship" Enterprise answering the phones, "Thank you for calling Enterprise, this is Paul, can I help you?" The name badge and the wrist band would be gone, but the sense of identity and mission would be a little sharper than it was before those days and nights in San Antonio.

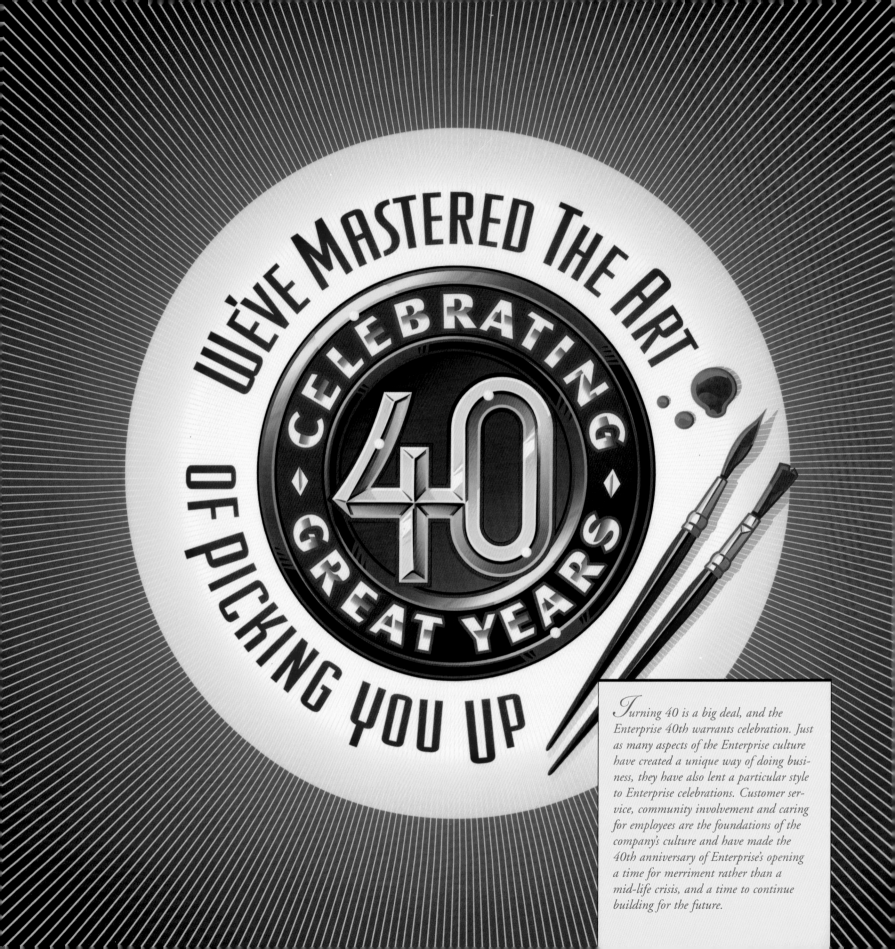

WE'VE MASTERED THE ART OF PICKING YOU UP

CELEBRATING 40 GREAT YEARS

Turning 40 is a big deal, and the Enterprise 40th warrants celebration. Just as many aspects of the Enterprise culture have created a unique way of doing business, they have also lent a particular style to Enterprise celebrations. Customer service, community involvement and caring for employees are the foundations of the company's culture and have made the 40th anniversary of Enterprise's opening a time for merriment rather than a mid-life crisis, and a time to continue building for the future.

Chapter Fifteen

NEW IDEAS AFFIRM A SOLID VISION

Thousands of hard-working, smiling people have taken Enterprise on a stratospheric journey from the basement of Forest Cadillac to the heights of the corporate world, all in the short space of 40 years. That first staff of seven has grown to a worldwide staff of over 30,000. That initial investment of $100,000 by Jack Taylor and the Lindburgs is now a company with assets totaling over $5 billion. The beginning rental fleet of 17 cars in 1962 has become a fleet of over 330,000 cars in more than 3,000 locations in three countries.

As the company crosses its 40-year mark and positions itself for the 21st century, the core Enterprise businesses — rental, leasing, car sales — all have promising futures.

Rental managers in the United States are pushing hard to build business with discretionary rental customers in local markets. This business, like the replacement business 20 years ago, has untapped potential. Overseas, rental managers are changing the way insurance companies and body shops view Enterprise, and business continues to grow rapidly. The dramatic success of the international expansion efforts in Canada and in England demonstrates that the Enterprise formula can cross national barriers and be successful.

The leasing business is growing steadily with its renewed focus on what Enterprise does best. The fleet business for small, commercial customers plays to the Enterprise strengths of customer service and local presence.

Car sales, a business where Jack was the pioneer in setting fixed prices for used cars, has also spread its wings as a national strategy. The continually increasing fleets of cars within the Enterprise system assure a constant supply of cars to be sold. At the same time, the world of used car sales has come around to Jack's way of thinking. Numerous competitors now offer fixed-price used cars, and consumers have begun to realize that this way of buying a car has its advantages.

And yet, the more things change, the more they stay the same. Treating people fairly has become ingrained as the guiding principle. That stays the same. Raise the bar for your own performance. That stays the same. Hustle. That stays the same.

As the core businesses continue to grow, Enterprise managers are constantly on the prowl for new ideas. How to do more business, how to do it better, how to do it differently are issues in the minds of Enterprise managers around the world. They continue the well-established process of taking measured risks, and when the risks work, they invest heavily to get the maximum impact. While the basic beliefs about how the company does business stay the same, the markets in which the company works keep presenting new challenges; cities from St. Louis

In 1993 Enterprise broke ground for its new corporate headquarters in St. Louis. Not far from the place where it all began, the new facility was designed to take the company forward into the next century. This facility represents forward movement that is well-grounded both in the original philosophy of Jack Taylor and in the modern technology of today.

This small trowel used at the groundbreaking is symbolic of countless small steps that have moved the company to a preeminent position in the business world.

As an international company reaching beyond U.S. borders, Enterprise chose to come back to its roots in Clayton to build its new home. At the 1993 groundbreaking were, from left to right, St. Louis County Executive Buzz Westfall; St. Louis City Mayor Freeman Bosley, Jr.; Andy Taylor; Jack Taylor; and Clayton Mayor Ben Uchitelle. The new structure brings together diverse Enterprise functions in one place, enabling the team to continue working closely together even as it gets bigger and better.

New Ideas Affirm a Solid Vision

FREE ENTERPRISE

JUNE/JULY

CELEBRATING DIVERSITY

1996 EMPLOYEE OPINION SURVEY RESULTS

When Jack Taylor founded Enterprise, everybody was in one small shop and talked together every day. Today, with thousands of locations in different parts of the world, internal communication takes more effort and requires different means. Technology has made e-mail an important tool, and the internal publication, Free Enterprise, *helps update employees on company issues.*

have been dreamed of in the basement of Forest Cadillac 40 years earlier.

"I am immensely proud of our company," says Andy Taylor. "It has become a wonderfully diverse team of people. They respect each other, and they respect the competition. But most of all, they want to win. My role is like a player-coach, a guy who is not only mapping out the game plan, but also out there on the field. I love watching these people execute the day-to-day details and putting it all together in a first-rate victory for the whole team."

The St. Louis mechanic who called Andy "the brave" many years ago would now be pleased to call Andy "the chief." From the time he was a teenager, Andy was intent on learning the

business, and learning it from the bottom up. What he inherited from Jack was tenacity and determination, not a predestined seat in a corner office.

Andy is also a planner and a worrier — he wants things to be right. Having things turn out right takes work, and Andy sets the tone for the future by making clear that it will take hard work — lots of it, from many people — to chart new strategies and plans. But he also makes clear that any new endeavors will be well grounded in the foundation that has been built customer by customer and employee by employee, treating others as one would like to be treated.

Throughout the Enterprise history, the stories demonstrate that it has been the people who have made the business exceed all expectations. They have worked hard, but many companies are full of hard-working people whose cumulative successes never hit the top of the charts. The Enterprise team has consistently gone beyond what was expected because they have believed in themselves. But of even

to Liverpool are all calling for new responses to a changing business environment.

In spite of the promising prospects for the current business, however, the most important future paths for Enterprise are paths not yet taken. History makes clear that Enterprise's ventures into new types of business have worked well, with only a few glitches along the way. The rock-solid strategic plan in place today could never greater importance, they have believed in the team of which they are a part.

Perhaps these Enterprise people in white button-down shirts (and a few aloha shirts) and neat dresses really are missionaries. They convert newcomers to believe that they can realize their dreams, they can push the limits and win, both for themselves and for the team. They continue to pull up an extra chair at the Enterprise table and welcome those who share the values of the Enterprise family. When they seek a competitive challenge, it is not just for the sake of beating a competitor, but to raise the bar they set for their own performance.

Their hopes for the future are partly for things they can see — higher-level jobs, new places to work and live, additional compensation. But they also have hopes for things not seen. They line up to join the team that will take Enterprise across the unknown frontier of the twenty-first century, sure that they want to be a part of it, unsure exactly what it will look like.

The Taylor family has changed over the 40 years since Jack founded the company. Jack and Mary Ann divorced in the late 1970s. Some years later Jack married Susan Orrison. They spend their time in St. Louis and in Florida, where they travel on his boat. Jack continues to enjoy his work at Enterprise, and the close-knit network of Enterprise friends still gets much of their attention.

Andy and Barbara have three daughters, Kelly, Chrissy and Patty, and Jo Ann has two daughters,

Tall tales and fish stories — who really caught the biggest fish? — are ties that bind many of the Enterprise people together as friends as well as business colleagues. They form one team, a team of distinctly different individuals who all function smoothly (most of the time) for a common purpose. These area rental managers from South Florida, here savoring their moment in the sun, all moved on to greater responsibilities at Enterprise.

New Ideas Affirm a Solid Vision

Fun in the sun is not limited to Florida. These members of the Enterprise Arizona team took a short outing to Mexico. The rest and relaxation was made more fun by using the vehicle on the right, not standard issue from the Enterprise fleet. Jack and Susan Taylor have continued to maintain close ties with many members of the Enterprise family.

Carolyn and Alison. The family ties are close, and the commitment of the Taylor family to the business is as strong today as it was in 1957. They retain profits in the business so that the growth can continue, and they oversee the constant reinvestment in the people of the company and in the communities in which they do business.

From his earliest days in business, Jack always wanted to be both boss and friend to the people who worked with him. Everybody was on a first-name basis with him — he called even the

newest employees by their first names, and he expected them to call him Jack.

As the team grew larger and larger, his instant recall for the name that went with each face became tougher. "Sport" became the standard nomenclature for everyone, and it came to signify both familiarity and a spirit of closeness and fun. Countless conversations and lunches ended with "Okay, Sport, thanks. I've got to go."

That parting phrase meant that he had learned whatever he needed to learn from that person, and now he was ready to move on. It also meant, "Get back to work." More often than not, he had been the one to ask the leading questions, and when he got up from the lunch table his plate was

*P*art of the 40th anniversary celebration involves looking at the company's beginnings while acknowledging work done by young artists today. This fleet of cars includes one car from each of the five decades during which Enterprise has been doing business. The cars are a 1957 Chevrolet Bel Air, a 1960 Cadillac, a 1971 Monte Carlo, a 1982 Camaro Z-28 and a 1997 Tahoe. They were decorated by artists who created designs to reflect the style of the decade during which each particular car was popular. The stenciled designs were transferred to vinyl and wrapped around the car, creating an entirely new interpretation of the Enterprise "wrapped" car.

*T*he designs, which were done in stencil by the artists, allow for a "paint-by-numbers" approach to completing the work so that many people can participate in the final product. Andy Taylor and Don Ross applied the initial paint to get the cars ready to roll.

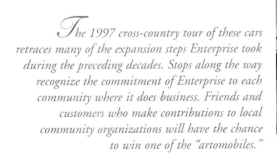

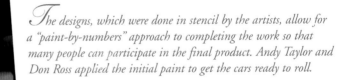

*T*he 1997 cross-country tour of these cars retraces many of the expansion steps Enterprise took during the preceding decades. Stops along the way recognize the commitment of Enterprise to each community where it does business. Friends and customers who make contributions to local community organizations will have the chance to win one of the "artomobiles."

New Ideas Affirm a Solid Vision

COMMANDING OFFICER
USS ENTERPRISE (CVN 65)

20 May 1997

Dear Mr. Taylor,

Thank you for your kind letter. It was a pleasure reading your father's sea stories from the seventh ENTERPRISE (CV 6). You can be assured that our Sailors today are proudly carrying on the tradition of ENTERPRISE excellence which has been passed on from former shipmates like your dad.

Please accept this note as an open invitation to visit ENTERPRISE anytime that is convenient for you and your father. It would be an honor to host both of you, and our Sailors would enjoy meeting you and showing you what they do. We are currently undergoing a brief maintenance period at Newport News Shipbuilding. My public affairs officer, Lieutenant Commander Denny Moynihan, will contact your office as soon as our underway schedule is confirmed.

Congratulations on celebrating 40 years of success in the car rental industry. Hope to see you soon on our ENTERPRISE.

Sincerely,

M. D. MALONE
CAPT   USN

Mr. Andrew Taylor
Enterprise Rent-A-Car
600 Corporate Park Drive
St. Louis, MO 63105-4211

Enclosure

The caps below were sent to Jack and Andy from the U.S.S. Enterprise. *The letter from the commanding officer of one* Enterprise *to the chief executive of the other* Enterprise *refers to "the tradition of* Enterprise *excellence which has been passed on...." It is that tradition of excellence that saw Jack and Andy Taylor through times of smooth sailing and times of very rough seas. They often asked others for ideas, suggestions and different points of view. But their leadership was unwavering, and the ship moved steadily forward.*

business and his fun in doing business have spurred on his team throughout the years. Enterprise people continue to call him and tell him the always hard-to-believe stories about life in a new city, opening a new branch and the latest adventures in the realm of customer service. He listens intently and loves to hear their stories.

Jack laughs at the unexpected tales his people tell, and when the stories are over, he sits up straight in his chair and gets ready to end the conversation. He straightens his glasses and says, "Okay, Sport. Keep at it. I'm meeting somebody for lunch. Got to go."

clean and the other plate had scarcely been touched. Many a cold lunch was left behind by the one who had been answering Jack's questions while Jack nodded and ate.

Even when people went away hungry, they felt replenished. In the process of answering questions, they had been encouraged just by his asking questions of them. When they went back to

work, there was renewed energy in their minds, even if it meant feeling the need for an early dinner to fill their empty stomachs.

Jack's vision has nurtured the Enterprise spirit and laid the groundwork for Andy's carefully crafted plans for the future. Jack's constant curiosity about the

Andrew Taylor —
From one great
Enterprise to another, congrats
on 40 years of excellence

[signature]
Captain
USS ENTERPRISE

𝒯*he engines are humming and the crew is well trained. With four decades of experience under their belts, team Enterprise moves deliberately and confi-dently ahead. The tentative steps out of that first basement office and into the heady daylight of the world around them paid off. Day by day and city by city, they built a force to be reckoned with, a powerfully competitive team that plays by the rules and pushes relentlessly for victory after victory.*

New Ideas Affirm a Solid Vision

TIMELINE

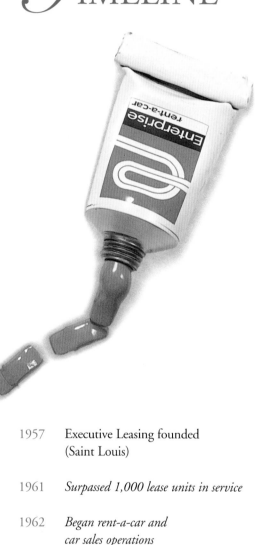

1957   Executive Leasing founded (Saint Louis)

1961   *Surpassed 1,000 lease units in service*

1962   *Began rent-a-car and car sales operations*

1964   *Surpassed $5 million in total assets*

1967   *Surpassed $10 million in total assets*
Surpassed $1 million in annual revenues
Introduced now-famous "Roadway E" logo

1969   *Surpassed 5,000 lease units in service*
Expanded beyond Saint Louis as Enterprise Leasing
Atlanta Group opened

1971   Orlando Group opened

1972   Kansas City Group opened
Tampa Group opened

1973   *Surpassed 1,000 rental units in service*
Houston Group opened

1974   Jacksonville Group opened
Keefe Supply Co. acquired

1975   South Florida Group opened

1977   *Surpassed 10,000 lease units in service*
Surpassed $50 million in total assets
Mexican Inn Chili Products acquired

1978   *Surpassed $50 million in annual revenues*
Executive Leasing (Saint Louis) changed to Enterprise Leasing
Indiana Group opened

1979   Colorado Group acquired
Dallas Group opened

1980   *Surpassed 5,000 rental units in service*
Surpassed $100 million in total assets
Courtesy Products acquired
National Reservations Center opened
San Francisco Group opened
Southern California Group acquired

1981   *Surpassed $100 million in annual revenues*
Phoenix Group opened

1982   *Surpassed 10,000 rental units in service*
Mexican Inn Chili Products divested
New Orleans Group opened
Southwest Group opened

1983   *Surpassed 100 offices*
Chicago Group opened

1984   *Surpassed 20,000 rental units in service*
Surpassed $250 million in total assets
Monogramme Confections acquired
North Texas Group opened
South Texas Group opened
Southeast Group opened
West Group opened
Washington D.C. Group opened

1985   *Surpassed $250 million in annual revenues*
Philadelphia Group opened

1986   *Surpassed 30,000 rental units in service*
Surpassed 20,000 lease units in service
Baltimore Group opened
Crawford Supply opened
ELCO Chevrolet acquired
Minnesota Group opened

1987   *Surpassed 40,000 rental units in service*
Surpassed $500 million in total assets
Detroit Group opened
South-Central group opened
Virginia Group opened

1988   *Surpassed 50,000 rental units in service*
Surpassed 500 offices
Surpassed $500 million in annual revenues
Enterprise Cellular acquired
New York Group opened

1989 *Enterprise Leasing changed to
Enterprise Rent-A-Car*
*Launched US national
advertising campaign*
Boston Group opened
Pittsburgh Group opened
Sacramento Group opened
Tennessee Group opened

1990 *Surpassed 100,000 rental
units in service*
Surpassed 30,000 lease units in service
Surpassed $1 billion in total assets
*Introduced now-famous
wrapped car trademark*
Hartford Group opened
Oregon Group opened
Pennsylvania Group opened
Seattle Group opened

1991 *Surpassed $1 billion in annual revenues*
Surpassed 1,000 offices
SNI Sports Network acquired
Bluegrass Group opened
Greater Michigan Group opened
Northern Ohio Group opened
Southern Ohio Group opened
West Virginia Group opened
Wisconsin Group opened

1992 *Surpassed 150,000 rental
units in service*
Surpassed $1.5 billion in total assets
Surpassed $1 billion in annual revenues
Heartland Group opened
Providence Group opened
Upstate NY Group opened
Utah/Idaho Group opened

1993 *Surpassed 200,000 rental
units in service*
Surpassed 1,500 offices
Monogramme Confections
merged into Courtesy Products
Expanded beyond the
United States (to Windsor)
Betallic Balloon acquired
Dakotas/Nebraska Group opened
Mountain Group opened
Ottawa Group opened
Southwest Ontario Group opened
Toronto Group opened

1994 *Surpassed 250,000 combined
rental and lease units in service*
Surpassed 2,000 offices
Surpassed $3 billion in total assets
*Surpassed $1.5 billion
in annual revenues*
*Recognized as largest (fleet and
locations) car rental company in U.S.*
*Expanded beyond North America
(to London)*
Alberta Group opened
British Columbia Group opened
Central Canada Group opened
Hawaii Group opened
Southeast England Group opened

1995 *Surpassed 250,000 rental units
in service*
Surpassed 40,000 lease units in service
Surpassed 2,500 offices
Atlantic Canada Group opened
The Bernard Company acquired
Enterprise Cellular divested
Montreal Group opened
Quebec City Group opened
SNI divested

1996 *Surpassed 300,000 rental
units in service*
Surpassed 50,000 lease units in service
Surpassed 3,000 offices
Surpassed $5.5 billion in total assets
Surpassed $3 billion in annual revenues
Birmingham Group opened
Cambridge Group opened
East Midlands/Nottingham
Group opened
Leeds/Bradford Group opened
Manchester/Liverpool Group opened
Monogramme Confections divested
Newcastle Group opened
Oxford/South Hampton
Group opened
Southwest England Group opened

1997 *Surpassed 350,000 rental
units in service*
Surpassed 60,000 lease units in service
Dusseldorf Group opened
Ireland Group opened
Munich Group opened
Scotland Group opened
Wales Group opened

189

ACKNOWLEDGMENTS

My first contact with Enterprise was a telephone call with a rental manager after an unfortunate collision which put my car in the repair shop. "Can I stop by with the car and pick you up?" he asked very politely. I was puzzled, and, to put it mildly, skeptical. To me, customer service was most often a computer generated post card I could return to let somebody know if my hotel room had been properly cleaned or my lunch served on time.

I soon discovered that the Enterprise version of customer service was different from anything I had experienced elsewhere. Several years later when I met Jack and Andy Taylor to discuss this book, I was intrigued to figure out how they had done it. How had these two very friendly men built a huge, successful company based on what seemed to be some simple concepts about how one should treat other people?

It was the vision of Jack and Andy that built Enterprise, and it was their vision that brought this book to life. I am grateful for their support and their constant attention both to our final objective of a good book and to the details necessary to make it happen. It has been rewarding and fun.

Steve Smith was always handy when I hit a tough spot and needed more information. Who was around when one thing or another happened, who knows good stories that describe the culture, who can help explain the connections between the company's growth and its culture? Steve was my guide through Enterprise history.

Thanks to the wonderful efforts of Nikki Lugo, the history of the company is told in pictures as well as words. By climbing through attics, garages and countless boxes she has pulled together the photographs and illustrations which help tell the story. Her work has helped bring the story to life.

I am particularly grateful for the assistance of Bronwyn Evans at Greenwich Publishing Group. Her role as editor understates the significance of her help. She was a sounding board in the early stages in helping to craft the flow of the story. Later, her efforts in refining the story and making sure we had our facts in order were immensely useful.

190

$\mathscr{I}$NDEX

All bold listings indicate an illustration.